TESTIM

As a small business owner, having access to knowledgeable advisors is critical. In terms of financial guidance, Derek excels at communicating complex information clearly. He prioritizes developing informed clients who may be partners in financial decision-making. Thanks to Derek, I understand the difference between a traditional and a Roth IRA and the benefits of each and much more. *Just Retire Already* brings Derek's lighthearted wisdom to all readers. He clarifies complex topics, while maintaining a friendly, accessible tone. The analogies he uses are relatable and the combination of text and visuals supports multiple learning styles. I highly recommend *Just Retire Already* to anyone who wants to increase their financial literacy and improve the likelihood of a comfortable stress-free retirement.

Barbara Wilson Arboleda, MS CCC-SLP
Entertaining Diversity, Inc. / Voicewize

I love the style of writing. It's almost conversational but not overly so. It's like I'm sitting down with someone and having them walk me casually through things so well I didn't even stop to realize this stuff was supposed to be horribly complicated.

Christopher Brescia, CEO
Fresh Tech Consulting

As an estate planning attorney, I see the sad consequences of failing to plan nearly every day. The first thing that America needs is a "wake up" call, and this book is it. America is not prepared to age. Our personal finances are not prepared to cover long-term care costs, which may easily exhaust a family's entire life savings. And budget deficits and taxes are only going to make the problem worse.

Derek is the right person to wake America up. All of the outstanding content I've seen him produce through various channels—all combined into a book to guide America into aging—I could not imagine something more needed right now in America.

Zach Anderson, Estate Planning Attorney
Brodowski, McCurry, Miller & Hoekenschnieder

I have known and worked with Derek for almost a decade and his advice, direction, and guidance have been invaluable to my wife and my long-term financial planning. As with most people, I assumed my retirement would take care of itself, I mean I maxed out my 401K every year—isn't that all you need to do? Meeting Derek, hearing the reality of retirement planning, and learning what proper investing looks like truly opened my eyes to what I (we) would need when the time to move into La Boca Vista comes upon us—and more importantly, he gave us the tools we needed to be in control of that decision so we could make it happen on our time frame.

Learning the proper investment strategies for our lifestyle both now and for retirement is not something we could have known. Additionally, I always thought I would sort this stuff out on my own. I mean how hard may it really be to store away money for the future? Looking back now, it makes sense—my accountant does my taxes, my mechanic fixes my car, my electrician handles the wiring; so why would I not want a professional financial advisor to handle my retirement?

The tools and strategies discussed in this book, which of course will be slightly different for everyone, are like being readied for battle and ensuring you have the right armament to come out a winner.

David Schulze, Regional Vice President
Service Max

Having immersed myself in Derek Mazzarella's book on financial and tax planning, I can confidently say it's a game-changer in the realm of personal finance literature. This captivating book goes beyond the conventional approach, infusing financial planning with personal anecdotes and captivating examples that not only educate but also entertain. The author's wealth of knowledge shines through, making complex finance and tax strategies accessible to readers of all backgrounds. With a blend of wit, wisdom, and real-life experiences, this book reshapes our preconceived notions on financial planning, empowering us to make informed decisions that can optimize our financial well-being. It's a must-have for anyone who is serious about their financial decisions and status throughout and after their professional journey.

Rushab Kamdar, Founder & CEO
Think Business 360

This book is a gift for even the long-time business owner; Derek is seasoned in retirement planning and illustrates the details in thoughtful and easy to follow terms. Not only was this book informative and not dry as this topic can lend itself to be but it sent me into a tailspin because I never considered state taxes on retirement, and many other insights carried through these chapters. This book helped point out many blind spots in our financial planning, and tools to get ahead for retirement planning.

Emily Isenberg, Founder & Creative Director
Isenberg Projects

I had the pleasure of working with Derek for five years. We worked together on many financial plans, and I had the opportunity to witness his deep concern for our clients and their well-being. Derek's holistic financial knowledge, and sense of humor, put clients' financial worries at ease. The ability to instill confidence about the future, and retirement, is one of his inherent gifts as a financial planner.

Richard (Dick) Howell, Financial Advisor
The Bulfinch Group

Derek is well positioned to author a book about retirement. Beyond possessing the formal educational background associated with earning a Certified Financial Planner designation, his interpersonal communication skills are exceptional which serve as a basis to develop a reasonable and attainable financial plan for his client's evaluation and consideration. We are certain that his book will be written in a manner that is easy to understand and written in plain English which is just the way Derek explains his financial recommendations to his clients.

David Brede, Vice President
Liberty Bank

JUST RETIRE ALREADY

An Unconventional Retirement Guide

DEREK MAZZARELLA, CFP®

Publish Your Purpose
141 Weston Street, #155
Hartford, CT, 06141

The opinions expressed by the Author are not necessarily those held by Publish Your Purpose.

Ordering Information: Quantity sales and special discounts are available on quantity purchases by corporations, associations, and others. For details, contact the publisher at hello@publishyourpurpose.com.

Edited by: Nancy Graham-Tillman
Cover design by: Rebecca Pollock
Typeset by: Jetlaunch

ISBN: 979-8-88797-998-4 (hardcover)
ISBN: 979-8-88797-999-1 (paperback)
ISBN: 979-8-88797-071-4 (ebook)

Library of Congress Control Number: 2023914738

First edition, October 2023.

Publish Your Purpose is a hybrid publisher of non-fiction books. Our mission is to elevate the voices often excluded from traditional publishing. We intentionally seek out authors and storytellers with diverse backgrounds, life experiences, and unique perspectives to publish books that will make an impact in the world. Do you have a book idea you would like us to consider publishing? Please visit PublishYourPurpose.com for more information.

DEDICATION

This book is dedicated to my wife Nicole. Without your love, support, and being our children's favorite, this book would have never happened.

To my sons, Harrison and Benjamin, don't be afraid of doing something big.

CONTENTS

FOREWORD

After reading this book and looking back at my career as a public accountant, a financial analyst, and now a financial advisor over a 30-year journey, one thing stands out to me the most: individuals lack the diverse financial knowledge needed to excel. It seems to me the media, CNBC, Bloomberg, YouTube, and other sources of news focus too much on investing, trading, stock picking, and the markets. Furthermore, with the introduction of Robinhood and other trading apps, individuals are being herded down a potentially dangerous path. There is too much emphasis on the stock market and trading stocks. But the market is just one piece of the puzzle.

The average individual takes more time planning a wedding or vacation or picking a college for their children than learning about financial concepts that will help them get to the retirement they deserve. Without basic financial knowledge, the average individual is prone to make poor financial decisions.

I'm glad you're taking the time to pick up this book to build your financial knowledge base. There is so much more to financial freedom and obtaining a comfortable retirement. Derek lays out many financial tools in this book that will help build your road to retirement and complete your financial puzzle.

Derek Mazzarella is a certified financial planner at Gateway Financial Partners. Soon after Derek joined Gateway, he and I began having lengthy discussions around his expertise in financial planning. I came from a wire house where we focused on the markets, investing strategies, and gathering assets. Financial planning sort of took a back seat. Since working alongside Derek, I have incorporated many more aspects of financial planning into my practice. It has elevated my process and my clients' experiences.

I am honored to write this foreword and share how passionate Derek is about reaching people to educate and help them pave a path to a successful, less stressful retirement.

Trish Sauer
Financial Advisor, Gateway Financial Partners

PREFACE:
IT'S GO TIME

Sit back and imagine you're at the point in life where you can finally hang it up and retire. Your heart is pumping with excitement as you walk down the hallway to your boss's office to let them know the good news (for you, at least). You feel a wonderful sense of relief and jubilation, but also a tinge of anxiety. You worry that you may be too bored or wonder if people are *really* going to miss you at work. The thought, *Did I really save enough money to retire?* pops into your mind, but it quickly dissipates under the excitement.

Fast forward, and you're a couple of years into retirement. Life is good. You get to see the grandkids more than you thought you would, you've found a group of other retirees to spend your time with, and you've picked up a hobby you've been putting off for years because you never had the time.

Then you turn on the news one day and see flashing red all over the screen. The stock market had a bad day and dropped a few points. You don't think much of it at the time, but the next day the market is down again. The following day is the same thing—a flashing red screen. This time the stock market drops more significantly. By the end of the week, the market is down again with seemingly no end in sight. You think back to the dot com crash in 2000, the housing market crash of 2008, and the "everything is down" year of 2022, and you wonder how bad it will be this time. You think to yourself, *I only have so much money saved* and know you can't afford to lose it all. Going online to check your account, you see it's down double digits even with a more conservative portfolio. You decide that you can't bear to lose any more money, so you make the trades and move most of your money to cash. You breathe a sigh of relief because at least you've stopped the bleeding, and you tell yourself you'll get back in when the market and economy look more solid.

Over the next few weeks and months, the market continues to drop. You feel great about your move to cash. You lost some of your money, but not as much as the people who stayed in the market. Continuing to relish your retirement, you meet with friends, see family, and enjoy your hobbies. As the next few months go by, the market is starting to rebound, but the economy still looks iffy. You stay in cash.

Now over a year has gone by, and the economy is settling down and the market has roared back above previous highs. It's time to go back in the market. You still feel good. Overall, your account value is down, but you needed the money to live on and couldn't risk losing more. Your house is fully paid off since that was a major goal of yours, so you decide to put some of your money back in the market and invest mostly in bonds.

Over time, you notice your account dropping a little bit each month. It looks like you got back into the market too late. Interest rates are low, and the stock market isn't keeping pace with the amount of money you're taking out. You reached the age when you must take money out of your IRA. It's more than you need, but you must do it. Now you're paying more for Medicare and your taxes have increased. You look for ways to cut costs, but the prices of your necessities have been increasing and you're spending more on healthcare than ever before. Eventually you start slowly cutting out the fun things you've been doing in retirement. The house needs repairs, your health is getting worse, and you've lived much longer than you ever thought you would. Now you're scrimping by. You look back and think, *I did everything I was supposed to do. I saved in my company's retirement plan, invested in the stock market, reduced my market risk in retirement, and paid my house off early. I did everything right.*

How would you feel if your retirement looked like that? Unfortunately, most people are heading down that path, including the ones who've planned well. Alternatively, you may have an enjoyable, fulfilling, and financially stress-free retirement. I've helped numerous people retire over the years, and they often mention to me that having a plan for retirement makes them feel lighter. Through working together with them, I've been able to help clients save thousands of dollars on taxes in retirement, create consistent streams of income, navigate bad stock markets, and, most importantly, enjoy retirement.

Retirees face many challenges, and conventional financial wisdom is outdated at best. The key to having a successful retirement is understanding the financial risks retirees face so that you may learn how to combat them. In this book, I outline the same strategies and tools I use to help clients retire well.

INTRODUCTION:
ARE YOU THE GUY WITH
THE DUCKS?

I often joke with my friends and tell them I've never had a real job (at least after college). The summer before I started college, I worked in a warehouse doing repetitive and monotonous tasks. I'm sure some of you may relate. That was enough motivation for me to do well in school with the hope of finding a career. That plan was working until it was time to actually get a job. In college, my goal was to be a business consultant at one of the big firms, but I had zero luck getting in the door.

Most of my friends in college had jobs lined up early on in the second semester of our senior year, but I had no job prospects to speak of and was getting antsy. Eventually I went to a job fair and had an interview with Aflac. With the promise that I could set my own hours, run my own business, make six figures—and meet the duck—I was off. In reality, I worked more hours than most people, sold supplemental insurance, barely made $30,000 . . . and never met the duck. My father wasn't happy that I took a "job" with no benefits or salary. Most people thought I was crazy, and they were right.

A year and a half later, I decided it was time to move on. Selling supplement insurance, getting asked multiple times a day if I was the "duck guy," and making very little money was not on my vision board. Like many people, I was struggling financially and had no ability to save for retirement.

Serendipitously, a financial advisor in my networking group suggested I come work with him at his firm. I always had an interest in finance and learning about how money works, so I figured that, worst-case scenario, I'd be able to apply what I learned to my own finances in case I ever had to get a real job. In the beginning of 2009, right in the midst of the largest stock market crash of my lifetime, I had decided to become a financial advisor. I'm not sure timing was my best trait, but I was able to persevere through a horrendous economy and market and found a job that I was passionate about.

Since then, I've had thousands of conversations with clients about their financial priorities, concerns and fears, and future dreams. One day, I had a conversation that completely altered my perspective on both my financial practice and my personal life.

I had been a financial advisor for only a couple of years and was having a casual conversation outside of the normal work environment with someone who wasn't my client. Suddenly, he said, "My wife will be fine if I die." Since most people never want to even *think* about dying early, I thought his statement was unusual and a little surprising. I asked him to explain more, and he went on to tell me he had over half a million dollars saved in his 401(k) plan, he and his wife had some cash in the bank, and their house was fully paid off. They even bought a vacation home that year.

He was right to an extent. They had put themselves in a pretty good spot financially. However, I explained how his wife would be too young to access the 401(k) funds without paying taxes and a penalty. They still had at least ten more years before they were ready to retire, which would put too much of a strain on the 401(k) assets even if his wife were allowed to take distributions. Using the equity in the house would require taking out a loan. Selling a house is never a quick and easy process either. The only life insurance coverage he had was through work (half of which would have been taxed) and a small $50,000 personal policy. I suggested that when open enrollment comes, he buy as much life insurance as he could through work because he wouldn't have qualified for a personal life policy. We left that conversation, and I didn't know whether he took my suggestions seriously; not all people do.

A few months later, he became ill. He ended up in the ICU and stayed there for months. After getting better, then worse, he passed away. He was 57 years old.

I found out later that he did take my advice and purchased another $300,000 life insurance policy through his workplace. It wasn't what he should've had, but it was enough to give his wife the freedom to make choices. She didn't *have* to sell her house even though everyone was telling her to do so. She didn't *have* to stay at her job, so she had the ability and time to decide what she wanted out of the rest of her life.

That person was my father. To this day I'm very grateful that he took my advice seriously. I know the positive impact having extra life insurance has had on my mom. When someone you love is sick, the last thing you should have to worry about is your finances. Knowing you'll be taken care of financially is incredibly powerful, and it gave my mom the time to be at my father's side until the end.

As I've had the time to reflect on what happened, I've noticed a few things about my parents' finances: They did everything that conventional wisdom taught them to do. They saved into their 401(k) plan, had an emergency fund, met regularly with their accountant, made extra payments to their mortgage, and used that mortgage to put their children through college. They did everything they were supposed to do, but there were still a few things missing.

After my father's death, I began collaborating with my mom to build on the financial work she and my father had done. We made some changes to her financial approach by expanding the financial tools she was using. We focused on planning for now and later. Now my mom is happily retired. She gets to focus on what really matters to her (her grandkids) and not worry whether her money will run out.

I tell this story because the concepts I'm going to discuss are the same ones I've used not only with clients but with members of my family. As I've worked with clients over the years, I've repeatedly noticed similar themes unfold. When it comes to financial planning and having a successful retirement, conventional wisdom is letting many people down. Conventional wisdom only goes so far.

My father's passing taught me that the advice I give may be incredibly impactful. That event led me to my life purpose. It's why I'm a financial planner and is what drives me. I want my clients and the people I interact with to be healthy, wealthy, and fulfilled.

One of the fulfilling parts of being a financial advisor is seeing my clients' confidence grow along with their financial knowledge. As my practice has grown, I've realized that I may realistically impact only the people I'm in direct contact with. My reach is limited by my time, and therefore my impact is limited. I've asked myself, *How may I reach more people and create the most lasting impact?* My answer inspired me to write this book.

Overall, my goal for this book is to help you feel more confident in your retirement. I'll do that by helping you understand the different types of risks in retirement, how they can negatively impact you, what conventional wisdom says to do, and how you can use financial tools to better mitigate these risks. Financial jargon may be confusing, so I'll break down financial concepts with analogies, stories about our two friends Pat and Sam, and of course charts . . . so many charts.

One theme you may notice along the way is how inter-twined many of these retirement risks are. Finances operate much like an ecosystem; one change may have a ripple effect on other seemingly unrelated areas. For example, the types of accounts you save money into now may affect the cost of your Medicare later. Financial decisions rarely happen in a vacuum, so it's imperative to consider how one financial decision may impact your finances in other areas.

This book is designed to be a retirement resource. Feel free to mark the pages, go back and reread sections, and evaluate how you may mitigate each retirement risk in your life. As a warning, the next few chapters are going to make retirement seem nearly impossible because I'll be focusing on the various retirement risks first. Don't worry. After that, I'll give you all the tools you'll need to have the retirement you want.

CHAPTER 1

BACK IN MY DAY, WE JUST DIED

As with most things in life, retirements have evolved over the years, and they will continue to do so with ever-changing technologies, financial products, and lifestyles. If you look back at the history of retirement, you'll see there was never really a golden age for retirement. The fact is, we've all sucked at it for a few generations now. This current iteration of retirement is relatively new.

Retirement as a concept goes back to the Roman Empire. In 13 BC, Caesar Augustus implemented the first retirement package for legionnaires. If they served 20 years in the Roman legions and five years in the reserves, they would receive a sum equal to 13 times their annual earnings.[1] Retirement pensions didn't resurface until the Revolutionary War when Congress established pensions for soldiers.

American Express started the first private pension in 1875, but the pension plan only covered employees who were injured or worn out while working on the company's railroad. Even

---

[1] Vauhini Vara, "The Real Reasons for Pensions," *New Yorker*, December 4, 2013, https://www.newyorker.com/business/currency/the-real-reason-for-pensions.

as private pension plans started becoming more common over the years, there was still a belief that you would work until you died. If you did happen to make it to old age and couldn't work, you were expected to use family savings, seek help from your church, or be taken care of by your children.

Government-run pension plans for rank-and-file citizens didn't start until the 1880s, when then Chancellor of Germany, Otto von Bismarck, created the first version of the pension for those age 70 or older. In an effort to reduce youth unemployment, he paid for those 70 and older to leave the workforce. Eventually, other countries followed Germany's lead and created retirement programs for people aged 65 and 70.[2]

America didn't adopt a government-based pension system until 1935, when the Social Security Act was passed under Franklin D. Roosevelt out of the ashes of The Great Depression. America was experiencing the same problem of high unemployment among youth as Germany once had 50 years earlier, and The Great Depression exacerbated the situation. The Social Security Act set the retirement age at 65. In 1935, the life expectancy of the average American was just over 60 years old. If an American did make it to 65, they would live, on average, 12 more years.[3]

Over the next few decades, pensions continued to enrich their benefits to private employees, and the number of people covered by a private pension grew. In the 1970s, 26.3 million workers were covered by a private pension, which equated to about 45% of the working population.[4] The number of workers

---

[2] Michael McLeod, "The History of Retirement," The Fiduciary Group Investment Managers, February 26, 2021, https://www.tfginvest.com/insights/the-history-of-retirement.

[3] Georgetown University Law Center, "A Timeline of the Evolution of Retirement in the United States," Workplace Flexibility 2010 Memos and Fact Sheets 50, March 26, 2010, https://scholarship.law.georgetown.edu/legal/50/.

[4] Liz Davidson, "The History of Retirement Benefits," Workforce, June 21,

covered by a private pension plan stayed relatively consistent over the next couple of decades. In 1990, the percentage of workers covered by a pension dropped slightly to 43.

In 1978, the Revenue Act was passed, which introduced the 401(k) plan. The 401(k) plan is a defined contribution plan, meaning that employers must worry about only the money that they put into the plan while an employee is working for the company, not the money they pay out to the employees in retirement. As life expectancies continued to rise, pension plans became continuously burdensome for employers.

By the 2000s, most private employers offered only defined contribution plans, and pension plans mostly went by the wayside. The retirement burden had shifted from the employer to the employee. While 401(k) adoption didn't occur immediately, the invention of the 401(k) represented a sea of change in retirement planning. Now, employees are required to fund their own retirement (with the help of a company match in most plans), decide how they should invest their money, and figure out how to generate retirement income from that savings. Throw in an increasing life expectancy, and it's no wonder that most Americans struggle with retirement.

This history lesson is included here to give you an idea of how retirements have evolved over the years as well as show you that there was never really a retirement golden age. Even when private pensions were at their peak, less than half of Americans were covered by a pension.[4] The three-legged stool concept, in which a person could rely on social security, a pension, and their savings for retirement, wasn't available for most of the population. Americans are still having trouble saving enough for retirement.

The National Retirement Risk Index conducted a study indicating that 50% of households are at risk of not having

---

2016, https://workforce.com/news/the-history-of-retirement-benefits.

enough money to maintain their lifestyles in retirement.[5] Currently, one in four Americans don't have any retirement savings, and those between 55 and 64 years old have saved only enough to generate about $1,000 a month in retirement.[6]

We really don't have generational knowledge of retirement as we do in other areas, such as woodworking or farming. Those skills and knowledge bases have been passed by for centuries, but retirement planning hasn't. Realistically, only two generations have retired, and one of them—baby boomers—is retiring right now. With the drop in private pensions, different markets, and changes in technology, retirements are vastly different among generations; one generation's advice may no longer apply. This may be one of the instances when it's OK not to listen to our parents.

If we just look at how interest rates have changed over the years, we may see how retirements are different for each generation. The Greatest Generation retired in the late '70s and '80s when interest rates were above 10%. We could invest in a CD back then and earn stock-market-like returns without the risk. We'd be lucky if we could earn more than 2%with a CD today. It's no wonder we suck at this.

The best way to solve this retirement issue is to save early, save often, and shoot for saving at least 15% of your income between a mix of retirement and investment accounts. The more money you save for retirement, the larger margin for error you have to handle the various retirement risks. However, simply saving gobs of money isn't a cure-all for retirement.

---

[5]   Alicia H. Munnell, Anqi Chen, and Robert L. Silciano, "National Retirement Risk Index: An Update from the 2019 SCF," *Center for Retirement Research at Boston College*, no. 21-2 (January 2021), https://crr.bc.edu/wp-content/uploads/2021/01/IB_21-2.pdf.

[6]   "Retirement in America: Time to Rethink and Retool," PricewaterhouseCoopers, accessed January 16, 2022, https://www.pwc.com/us/en/industries/financial-services/library/retirement-in-america.html.

Even if a person is considered a good saver, there are still risks that may derail a retirement. Understanding how to alleviate these risks is critical for a successful retirement and will put less pressure on your savings to last throughout your retirement years.

Financial planning and retirement planning are all about creating small wins that add up over time and will ultimately make a significant impact. At the end of the day, I don't want your retirement plan to be, "I'll just die."

CHAPTER 2

WHEN DID ALL THESE ROBOTS GET HERE?

Financial advisors look at retirement differently from other people. Most people have the understanding that they need to save a certain amount of money and then their retirement will be fine. The most common question I get from clients is, "How much do I need to save for retirement?" The truth is, there is no magical retirement number.

Financial advisors are trained to always look at the "what ifs" in life. What if you die early? What if you get sick and can't work any longer? What if inflation gets out of control? What if Adele never records a new album?! It's a difficult way of looking at the world. We do it not because we like it, but because our clients typically don't, and we want to make sure they're financially prepared for difficult life events.

We help our clients navigate retirement the same way. Looking at what may derail a retirement, we plan for various outcomes. The truth is, retirement is an ever-evolving experience. Financial advisors don't know how long a client's retirement will last or how the world will change over the course of a person's retirement. Think about how much has changed in the past 25 years. Back then there were no smart phones, streaming services, or robot vacuums. Advisors from the 1990s didn't model any of these expenses into retirement plans, but they are a part of our everyday lives now. Think about how many subscription services you're currently paying for.

We financial advisors tackle this problem by mapping out various scenarios for their clients. To do this, one of the tools we utilize is a Monte Carlo simulation, a mathematical model that may simulate a person's retirement one thousand or more times and potentially predict a potential success rate for their retirement based on various factors. If the simulation predicts someone will have enough money for retirement nine hundred out of the one thousand times, that person's potential success rate will be 90%. In essence, a financial advisor may use a Monte Carlo simulation to evaluate the riskiness of a person's portfolio, the amount of money they project to retire with, the different market conditions, how much a retiree spends, the impact of taxes, and more. It may suggest how a person's retirement would look whether the stock market does well or doesn't.

Refer to figure 1 for an illustration of a sample Monte Carlo simulation. You'll see the wide range of returns at the top, and the bottom represents essentially best- and worst-case scenarios. The more likely outcomes are represented within the darker shaded area on the graphic. The bottom of the chart shows the potential success rate by percentage, up to 100%. The further along the lines go, the higher potential success rate a retiree has. In figure 1, this hypothetical retiree has a potential success rate of 91%.

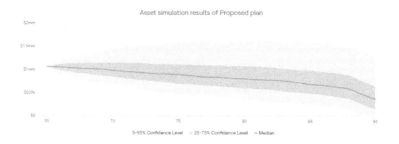

Figure 1: Sample Monte Carlo Analysis. "Knowledge Base: Monte Carlo Scenario Generation," RightCapital Help Center, accessed February 6, 2023, https://help.rightcapital.com/article/126-monte-carlo-scenario-generation.

Monte Carlo simulations aren't the end-all and be-all, and they certainly have their flaws, but they do give financial advisors a good idea about whether a retiree is making a decision that's moving them in the right direction. For example, if an advisor sees that saving into a Roth IRA over a traditional IRA increases a client's potential success rate from 85 to 90%, that advisor feels confident that saving into a Roth IRA is the better financial decision. Retirement may be emotional, and it's helpful to leverage math when making financial decisions.

The point of explaining all this is that while most people believe retirement is all about maximizing returns and reaching for the highest ceiling, financial advisors look at raising the floor. We ask ourselves how we may eliminate the bad things that may ruin a retirement so that, no matter what happens, a retiree won't run out of money. Raising the floor often means integrating less sexy financial products, discussing what may go wrong, and building a plan for various outcomes. Instead of focusing on maximizing returns and assets, retirees need to transition their thinking toward using their assets to generate the most income.

If you want to understand how to raise the floor, you first must recognize the retirement risks. Only then may you devise a strategy to diminish them. The strategies I'll be discussing with you have been evaluated through the lens of raising your floor and lowering your stress. I've been implementing them with active clients and have tested them through Monte Carlo analysis. Keep in mind that not all the upcoming strategies will be a fit for you. My goal is to bring your attention to them so you may think about your retirement from a different perspective and figure out what strategies are best-suited for you.

CHAPTER 3

BUY! BUY! BUY! SELL! SELL! SELL!

Let's say you're a farmer and you know you need a certain amount of water every year to ensure that your crops grow. If you use too little water, your crops may not survive. If you use too much water, you may drown your crops. Your only water source is a well, and there needs to be enough rain each year to refill it.

What if a drought comes one year? You still need to use the same amount of water for your crops. Eventually there's some rain, but it's not enough to refill your well. You may get by this year, but if you don't get enough rain moving forward, you could eventually be in trouble. If you're not prepared, the only options are to reduce the number of crops you grow or pay for water elsewhere. Either way, a lack of rain means you may not make enough money to keep your farm.

Similarly, if your investment returns are too low for too long, you may end up with a worse retirement than expected. The occasional rain is your investment return, and your well is your retirement portfolio. To get enough money flowing when your well is running dry, you may choose to either spend less in retirement (reduce the number of crops you grow) or take on more risk (pay for water elsewhere).

An old adage about the stock market that sounds incredibly simple and somewhat obvious is, "Buy low and sell high," meaning buy stocks when their value is depressed and sell them when everyone else gets in too late for a sweet profit. Buying low and selling high sounds simple enough, but studies have shown that it's nearly impossible to correctly time the market. In fact, over the last 20 years, the average investor has returned only 2.9% per year on average.[7] By comparison, that's a worse return than many singular asset classes such as real estate investment trusts (REITs), emerging market equities, small caps, high yield bonds, the S&P 500, a 60/40 portfolio,[8] developed market equities, bonds, houses. . . it's a long list. While you may yet be unfamiliar with what these assets are, the point here is to illustrate that the average investor doesn't execute the "buy low and sell high" strategy well. Emotion often takes over, and most investors do the opposite: buy high when the market goes up and sell low when the market drops.

Luckily, market fluctuations don't matter as much when you're consistently saving money as you would do with a 401(k) plan. When the market drops, people buy more shares and gain more value, and when the market increases, they buy fewer shares. Eventually, this continuous investing process helps even out stock market fluctuations. This is one of the rare times when putting your head in the sand works well.

Pre-retirees have one other thing going for them: time. When they're saving for retirement, they have time on their side. They may weather a bad market by not overreacting and

---

[7] "Guide to the Markets," J. P. Morgan Asset Management, last modified December 31, 2022, https://am.jpmorgan.com/content/dam/jpm-am-aem/global/en/insights/market-insights/guide-to-the-markets/mi-guide-to-the-markets-us.pdf.

[8] A 60/40 portfolio is an investment portfolio made up of 60% stocks and 40% bonds. Conventional wisdom often utilizes a 60/40 portfolio as the standard asset mix for a retiree.

selling at a loss. If they stay invested, the stock market eventually rebounds and will surpass the previous market highs, rewarding their patience.

Retirees don't have the luxury of time. What do they do when they *need* to sell after the market drops by 25% and can't wait for the stock market to rebound?

Taking money from your investments during a market loss exacerbates the loss and puts excess pressure on your portfolio to perform better than average moving forward. As a retiree, you have two choices with your portfolio: take on more risk or invest more conservatively. Taking on more risk in your portfolio may help you eventually make up the loss, but it increases the likelihood of a more significant loss when another market correction occurs. Shifting to more conservative investments after a loss is the equivalent of falling behind in a race and going slower to catch up. How's that going to work out for you?

To illustrate my point, let's use an example with small numbers. If you have $100 and then lose 10%, you now have $90. What return would you need to get back to $100? Most people would say 10%, but that would only get you to $99. Since 10% of $90 is $9, it would actually take an 11% return to get back to $100. Likewise, if you lose 20%, you must earn 25% back to break even. For reference, the Standard and Poor's (S&P) 500, an index that tracks the performance of the five hundred largest US companies to build a composite return, is often used as a shorthand when explaining what "the stock market does." Dating back to its inception in 1957, this index indicated earnings of 10.14% per year on average.[9] So while earning 25% in one year is possible, it isn't probable. The S&P

---

[9] Ian Webster, "Stock Market Returns Between 1957 and 2022," S&P 500 Data, accessed January 25, 2022, https://www.officialdata.org/us/stocks/s-p-500/1957.

500 has earned 25% or more only four times in the past 20 years.[10] Figure 2 shows what it would take to break even after a market drop.

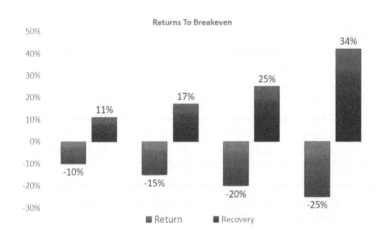

Figure 2: Returns Needed to Breakeven in Various Scenarios.

While a person accumulating assets has time for the market to get back to previous market highs, what happens when they must take out money during a market correction? The traditional safe withdrawal rate is considered 4%. Starting with the same $100, if you lose 15% *and* must withdraw 4% to cover your living expenses, your $100 is now down to $81. You'd have to earn 23.5% just to break even. If you earn the average 10% return, you're only back to $90, with another $4 to take out again. A market drop combined with retirement distributions may create a snowball effect. Throw in the reality that a retiree never takes out the same exact amount each

---

10   J. B. Maverick, "S&P 500 Average Return," Investopedia, last modified August 16, 2022, https://www.investopedia.com/ask/answers/042415/what-average-annual-return-sp-500.asp#toc-sp-500-historical-returns.

year because of unexpected expenses, major projects, etc., and you may start to see how a market correction feels different for retirees.

Figure 3 shows how much you would need to earn to breakeven if you added in a 4% withdrawal rate when that same market drops.

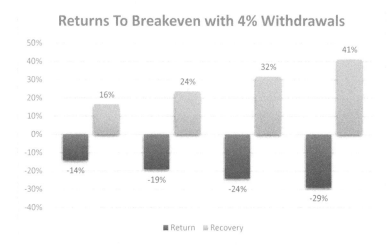

Returns To Breakeven with 4% Withdrawals

Figure 3: Returns Needed to Breakeven after 4% Withdrawal. This return scenario was created by the Author, Derek Mazzarella.

If your retirement account suffered even a 20% loss and you had to take 4% out, you'd need 31.6% to breakeven. How long would it take you to earn that? How may you possibly climb out of that hole? How would you *feel* about it? More importantly, how are you going to react to a market drop in retirement? An underrated aspect of market risk in retirement is the impact on human behavior. Most people wouldn't be able to stomach a significant market loss. People tend to feel a loss more than they enjoy a market gain. Are you the type of person to stay disciplined and not sell when the market drops?

Another item to consider is the frequency of market downturns. The average intra-year stock decline is 14.3%.[11] On average, a 10% drop occurs every 16 months, a 15% drop occurs approximately every 3.25 years, and a 20% drop occurs about every 5.5 years. If your retirement is 20 years long, you could potentially see three market drops of 20% or more. See table 1 for more detail.

Table 1. *History of Stock Market Decline Occurrences*

	-5% or More	-10% or More	-15% or More	-20% or More
Average Frequency	Roughly 3 times a year	About once per year	About once every 3.5 years	About once every 6.3 years
Length (Days)	43	110	251	370

Source: "What Past Stock Market Declines May Teach Us," Capital Group | American Funds, accessed May 27, 2022, https://www.capitalgroup.com/individual/planning/market-fluctuations/past-market-declines.html.

Note: Assumes 50% recovery of lost value. Length measures market high to market low.

All of this is to say that stock market returns will fluctuate over time. There will be periods of growth, and there will be periods of decline. Since withdrawals are already coming from a retiree's portfolio, periods of decline may affect a retiree more than a saver.

A market drop may be challenging for a retiree to pull themselves out of. For most retirees, the answer is to either take on more market risk to get back to their original balance or reduce their living expenses. Others may advise to simply have a more conservative portfolio. That may help reduce market risk, but as I'll get into in later chapters, being too conservative

---

[11]   Ian Webster, "Stock Market Returns."

may sometimes cause a retiree to run out of money due to various other factors. How will you go about refilling your well in retirement?

Chapter Highlights

- Stock markets will constantly fluctuate, and stock market drops of 20% or more happen about once every 5.5 years.
- The average investor returns about 2.9% per year, which is below that of an average 60/40 portfolio.
- It takes more to recover from market drops than percentage drops (e.g., a 10% drop needs an 11% rate of return to break even).
- Market drops are even more challenging for retirees since they are already taking withdrawals (e.g., a 15% drop would take 23.5% to recover from).
- Market drops combined with withdrawals may have a negative compound effect on retirement funds.

CHAPTER 4

HEY, I JUST GOT HERE!

This is going to date me, but the marketing for the movie *Scream* was all about Drew Barrymore. She was featured on the movie posters and all other marketing collateral. Going into the movie, I assumed she was going to be the lead actress. Then I went to see the movie and—spoiler alert!—she dies within the first ten minutes of the movie!

Sequence of returns risk is a little like that. There's a buildup to retirement, most people don't even know it exists, it happens early on in a person's retirement, and much like the beginning scene in *Scream*, sequence of returns may be jarring.

The basic concept of a sequence of returns is that two people may retire with the same amount of money, earn the same average rate of return per year over the course of their retirement, spend the same amount per year out of their portfolio, but have very different outcomes. One person's retirement may be considered successful, while the other person's retirement could be dramatically worse or even fail. Since most financial planning and portfolio return forecasting is done on an average annual return basis, retirees rarely see this coming. They assume it will be fine if their portfolio earns 6 or 7% in retirement, but real life doesn't work that way. In fact, the market rarely performs close to the average return on an annual basis.

Another way to think about sequence of returns risk is to consider your commute to work. If you've ever had a commute to work, there's one thing you know to be true: you have a window of time that you need to leave the house by, and if you miss the window and leave even five minutes later, you're going to be stuck in traffic and have a much longer and frustrating commute. You're driving the same car, going the same distance, and traveling on the same roads, but the outcome may be different based on leaving even a few minutes later. Sequence of returns risk is the same concept as the commute. How is this possible?

The difference lies in when the stock market decline occurs for a retiree. If a person retires into a good stock market, they'll likely have a more pleasant retirement. If a person retires into a down stock market, they may have to make concessions to their retirement, such as spending less. Sequence of returns risk is concerning since you may do everything you're supposed to do, but bad timing may significantly alter the enjoyment or success of your retirement.

Oddly enough, we spend so much time worrying about investing into the wrong market. We always want to get the timing right. The truth is that when it comes to long-term investing, the timing matters very little if we're saving consistently.

Table 2 illustrates that while our rides might be different, our end location is ultimately the same. It shows the growth of two S&P 500 return scenarios starting with $500,000 and investing $20,000 per year for 20 years. The gray line shows the actual returns of the S&P 500 from 2000 to 2020, and the black line shows the returns in reverse order. While both investment paths are different, they end up at nearly the same endpoint ($2,888,466 vs. $2,849,932). Whether you earn a higher return in the beginning doesn't matter as much when you're accumulating assets.

Table 2. *Impact of Sequence of Returns When Saving*

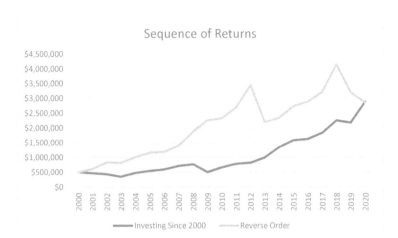

Source: Author, Derek Mazzarella, CFP.

As I've mentioned, taking in income while the market is dropping may have a negative effect on a person's overall portfolio. But what about the impact of *when* those negative returns occur? Let's compare two retirement scenarios.

Both start with $1,000,000 and take an annual withdrawal of $40,000 plus a 2.5% inflation rate each year. One person retires in 1999, and the other retires just one year later in 2000. If they had both invested in the S&P 500, the 1999 retiree would've been in great shape, ending up with almost as much money as they started with ($948,526) while taking distributions of $1,223,377.

The 2000 retiree had a much rougher retirement experience. They would've immediately seen three consecutive negative return years, resulting in their account value diminishing by almost half in 2003. By 2009, their portfolio was valued at under $400,000. The 2000 retiree would have over $600,000 less than the 1999 retiree, even though they had one fewer year of withdrawals. At what point would you have panicked? Table 3 illustrates the impact of sequence of returns risk.

Table 3. *Sequence of Returns in Retirement*

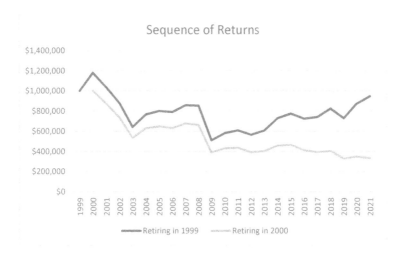

Source: Author, Derek Mazzarella, CFP.

You may be thinking to yourself, *But I won't have 100% of my money invested in the S&P 500*, and you're most likely right. Not many people would have their entire retirement allocated to stocks. So then how would the same scenario play out with a 60/40 portfolio?

Table 4 indicates that the difference between the two retirements isn't as drastic. The retiree from 1999 finishes with more money than they started with ($1,100,708), while the 2000 retiree finishes with $864,483. That's a difference of $236,225, and the 2000 retiree still took in less income ($1,223,377 vs. $1,154,514). That's still a lot of early bird specials they're leaving on the table.

Table 4. *Impact of Sequence of Returns on a 60/40 Portfolio*

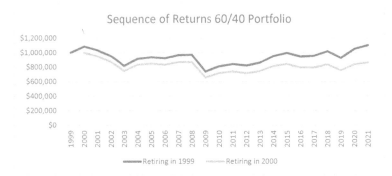

Sequence of Returns 60/40 Portfolio

Retiring in 1999   Retiring in 2000

Source: Author, Derek Mazzarella, CFP.

The point with sequence of returns risk is that although you may retire with the same amount of money and take out the same amount of money as another retiree, the market you retire into may have an impact on your retirement. Each market will be different. And what happens in a year like 2022 when both stocks and bonds are down in the same year?

The ultimate problem with sequence of returns risk is that you may do everything right and may still run out of money in retirement. Retirees used to be able to mitigate sequence of returns risk with pension plans, but those are rarely available anymore. Since it's nearly impossible to time the stock market, there's virtually no way to know what kind of market you'll retire into.

Chapter Highlights

- Sequence of returns risk is a stock market drop that happens within the first few years of retirement.
- Starting retirement in a down market may cause you to run out of money or adjust your spending, especially if

future stock market returns aren't good enough to help you recover the initial losses.

- Sequence of returns risk is a risk you have minimal control over.
- Average returns are not a reliable retirement income projection tool.

CHAPTER 5

HEALTHCARE COSTS— TAKE CARE OF YOUR BODY; IT'S WHERE YOU LIVE

I t's time to bring your car in for a routine oil change, so you leave it with a mechanic you trust. A few hours after dropping your car off, you get a call from your mechanic. Your brake rotors are shot and need to be repaired, and it's not safe to drive otherwise. The bill from the mechanic is well above what you expected to spend when you thought all you needed was an oil change. Unfortunately, you have no options because you need your car.

Long-term care may be like that in retirement. It often comes as an unexpected expense that ends up being much more than you had planned on spending. There are generally few alternatives. If you're not prepared for the unexpected expense, it may be financially devastating.

One of the lessons I've learned in life is that health is everything. Too often we're reactionary when it comes to our health. We see a doctor or go to a hospital only after we're sick. Outside of having health insurance, most of us never plan for being unhealthy. Every year, one or two people reach out to me to inform me they were just diagnosed with cancer and ask how they may get life insurance. Unfortunately, I have to tell them they can't get any; it's too late for them. Every time I do it, it's heartbreaking, and I feel helpless not being able to take care of them.

Most people treat medical care in retirement the same way. If a retiree is reactionary with their healthcare planning, it may not only ruin the enjoyment of their retirement but also be financially devastating. As a financial planner, I constantly see stats about the total cost of care in retirement. RBC Wealth Management conducted a study that found the average cost of care in retirement for a "healthy" 65-year-old couple is $662,156.[12] That doesn't even include the cost of long-term care. What is a retiree supposed to do with that number? Do they just set aside $662,000? We don't plan for things like a $4,647 retirement Netflix bill (yes, that is what you would spend on Netflix over 20 years if the cost never increased).

To help you understand healthcare costs in retirement, I should discuss two main costs: routine annual healthcare and long-term care. Routine care consists of health insurance premiums (most often Medicare) and out-of-pocket medical costs. Long-term care is a medical event that requires some form of medical assistance, whether that's in-home help or the use of a long-term care facility. Let's dig deeper into the two medical costs.

---

[12]   Angie O'Leary, Griffin Geisler, and Daniel Gottlieb, "Taking Control of Healthcare in Retirement," RBC Wealth Management, accessed March 8, 2022, https://www.rbcwealthmanagement.com/_assets/documents/insights/taking-control-of-health-care-in-retirement.pdf.

Routine Annual Healthcare

The main problem with retirement planning is that people tend to drastically underestimate the annual medical costs for a retiree. According to the same RBC study mentioned earlier, only 56% of people factored healthcare into their plans. They also believed the average annual out-of-pocket cost of care was $2,700, when in reality it is $6,100 per person per year in the United States.[13]

There are four items that affect healthcare costs in retirement: your current health status, your location, the type of medical plan you choose, and your income.

Health Status

Healthcare is very personal, and the cost of healthcare in retirement may vary based on a person's health. You may automatically assume that a healthier person would pay less for healthcare in retirement, but that's not necessarily the case. While an unhealthier person may pay more in the short term, a healthier person with a longer life span may ultimately pay more due to the ever-rising cost of healthcare. Essentially, the healthier retiree is paying less each year, but for a longer period of time.

Location

Healthcare costs vary widely depending on the state you live in. Medicare Parts A and B are the same throughout the country, but supplement coverage is different for each state. There's a fairly significant difference between the cheapest state and the most expensive state, the latter of which is more than twice that of the former.

---

[13]   O'Leary, Geisler, and Gottlieb, "Taking Control of Healthcare in Retirement."

Type of Medical Plan

The two main types of Medicare coverage are traditional Medicare and Medicare Advantage. Traditional Medicare typically offers more freedom of choice with doctors, while Medicare Advantage has lower premiums but greater restrictions on care. You may want a plan that covers more prescriptions or has a wider network of doctors. With medical coverage, you either pay more for premiums or pay more if/when something happens (out-of-pocket expenses). Talking to a Medicare specialist may help you determine the best coverage for you.

Income In Retirement

In retirement you may buy insurance through a private insurance carrier, or you may get medical coverage through Medicare. The cost of Medicare Part B will be based on your income. Higher-income earners pay more for Medicare compared to lower-income earners. To dig a little deeper, Medicare Part B coverage has six different cost tiers based on income. Moving from the lowest tier up just two tiers *doubles* your monthly premiums. The difference between the lowest cost tier and the highest is a 239% increase.[14]

To determine your Medicare income-related monthly adjustment amount (which is a fancy way of saying cost), the Social Security Administration will look back at the average of your last two years of modified gross adjusted income. This calculation will include any salary, business income, social security benefits, realized investment gains, and income/interest from investments (including tax-free income from municipal bonds). Only income from a Roth IRA, an HSA, a reverse mortgage, or a loan from a permanent life insurance

---

[14] "2023 Medicare Costs," Centers for Medicare and Medicaid, accessed March 8, 2022, https://www.medicare.gov/Pubs/pdf/11579-medicare-costs.pdf.

policy are excluded. As I'll discuss in a later chapter, figuring out a tax-efficient income-withdrawal strategy may lead to lower Medicare costs in retirement.

Quick Tip: Social security may provide an exception for their two-year income look-back rule. If there is a drastic change in your income, you may file form SSA-44 for an exception. One such exception is for a recent retiree. Instead of basing their income off their last two working years, retirees may file an exception to base their cost premiums on their retirement income.

LONG-TERM CARE

"If I get to that point, put a pillow over my face." I hear that phrase a few times a year. How about we just make a plan in case we get sick? Wouldn't that be a better option? Besides, my wife bought nice pillows and I don't want to ruin them.

When it comes to needing long-term care, the people in the "it's not going to happen to me" group are misguided. According to LongTermCare.gov, 70% of people aged 65 or older will need some form of long-term care services. Seven out of 10 people is a very high number, and it's something you must plan for. Would you swim in the ocean if there were a 7 in 10 chance of a shark attack? Long-term care costs too much, and the odds are too high to ignore it. On average, women need care for 3.7 years, and men need care for 2.2 years.[15]

The cost of long-term care services is a sliding scale based on a person's needs. Most care will start off in the home with a home health aide because many people prefer to stay in their home as long as possible. The next level up is community and

---

[15] "How Much Care Will You Need?" LongTermCare.gov, accessed March 8, 2022, https://acl.gov/ltc/basic-needs/how-much-care-will-you-need.

assisted living, which ranges from adult day care to more comprehensive assisted living. Nursing home care is the last stage and comes into play when a person needs full-time care. The costs of these services ramp up significantly as the need for care increases. Your location plays a major role in the cost as well.

Based on data from Genworth, table 5 outlines the various monthly costs in 2021 by service type and location, and table 6 shows the expected monthly costs for care in 2051 (with an assumed 4% inflation rate).

Table 5. *Monthly Cost of Care in 2021*

Location	In-Home: Home-maker	In-Home: Health Aide	Adult Day Care	Assisted Living	Semi-Private Room (Nursing Home)
National	$4,957	$5,148	$1,690	$4,500	$7,908
New York	$5,529	$5,720	$1,950	$5,750	$12,471
Arkansas	$4,185	$4,185	$1,733	$3,750	$6,083

Source: Genworth, "Cost of Care Survey," accessed March 8, 2022, https://www.genworth.com/aging-and-you/finances/cost-of-care.html.

Table 6. *Projected Monthly Cost of Care in 2051*

Location	In-Home: Home-maker	In-Home: Health Aide	Adult Day Care	Assisted Living	Semi-Private Room (Nursing Home)
National	$16,078	$16,697	$5,481	$14,595	$25,649
New York	$17,933	$18,552	$6,325	$18,650	$40,448
Arkansas	$13,574	$13,606	$5,621	$12,195	$19,730

Source: Genworth, "Cost of Care Survey."

As you may see from the tables, long-term care expenses may add up quickly. If you look at just the monthly national average cost of an in-home health aide in 2051 and project that over the average time long-term care is needed, a male would need $434,122 over 2.2 years to cover the cost, while a female would need $717,971 over 3.7 years. Where's that money going to come from?

If this wasn't made clear, let me say it clearly: healthcare in retirement is a significant expense. Per person, annual medical costs made of up insurance premiums and out-of-pocket expenses may be over $6,000 per year. Throw in a long-term care event, which is not only highly probable but also another potential six-figure plus expense, how prepared are you to cover these costs in retirement?

Chapter Highlights

- Medical expenses in retirement come in two ways:
- Annual medical premiums and out-of-pocket expenses
- Long-term care
- Medical expenses in retirement may average $6,000 per year, or over $662,000 for a couple over the course of retirement.
- Medical costs are based on health, location, type of medical plan, and income in retirement.
- There is currently a 70% chance that you may need long-term care in retirement.
- Long-term care comes in three phases: in-home care, assisted living, and facility care (nursing homes).
- Long-term care costs vary by state and the type of care needed.
- Medical care has a higher-than-average inflation rate.

CHAPTER 6

INFLATION—WHEN DID THESE BAGS OF CHIPS GET SO SMALL?

Anyone who's ever spent time with someone much older than them knows that person eventually tells stories about the "old days." They tell you how much tougher they had it, how much harder their generation worked, how everything was up a hill, and how much cheaper everything used to be. You might hear how they bought their first house for $30,000 or how they paid their way through college by working at a grocery store. This is my very roundabout way of saying that inflation is a part of life. Over time, the things we buy get more expensive.

A common story about frogs is that if you put one in a pot of water and turn on the heat, the frog won't realize that the water is getting hotter. The frog will only realize the water is hot once it's boiling, and at that point it's too late. That analogy describes inflation. The value of our accounts may not change, so we think we have the same amount of money. In reality, inflation means we may buy less of the same thing over time. If we don't pay attention to it, inflation may boil our retirements without us realizing it until it's too late.

Inflation is one of the silent killers of retirement. When we have a finite amount of something, it's in our human nature to try our best to preserve that something. Most retirees would prefer to be conservative with their money since they are no longer working and don't have an avenue to increase their nest egg. The fear of loss is why so many retirees put their money in cash or CDs. What they don't realize is that over time they're all but ensuring they will lose money. As the years go by, buying power decreases. Groceries that were once $100 a week are now $175 a week. The returns on cash or CDs aren't high enough to keep pace with growing costs. It's the reason your grandparents only had about five outfits and shag carpet for 35 years.

One other item to look at is how retirees spend money in retirement. Since every day is a Saturday for retirees, a variety of expenses often disappear for them, such as new work clothes and childcare-related expenses, and are replaced by new ones, such as vacations and home renovations (as well as increased healthcare expenses). Naturally you'd think inflation would be lower in retirement, but inflation tends to be worse for retirees. Let's see why that is.

How Inflation Hits Differently in Retirement

Whenever you hear about inflation in the news, you're usually getting the general inflation number, or consumer price index, which measures the increased costs of goods and services over time, such as the price of gas and airplane tickets. As a result, most planners will use the same general inflation numbers when projecting their future expenses. When you look at inflation in more detail, however, you'll see there are inflation rates for a variety of categories, such as healthcare, education, housing, and travel. When planning for inflation in retirement, retirees should match where they spend their time and money with that category's inflation rate.

Retirees spend less time working and more time socializing, engaging in leisure activities, and working on their houses. The top four spending categories for retirees are healthcare, housing (not including a mortgage), food and beverage, and transportation. By comparison, a pre-retiree's top four categories are housing, food and beverage, transportation, and mortgage.

Over the last 30 years, the average inflation rate has been 2.4%.[16] Table 7 illustrates inflation rates by spending category over a 36-year period.

Table 7. *Inflation Rate by Spending Category, 1982–2018*

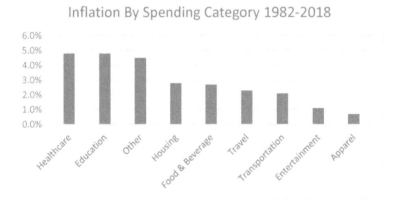

Source: "Databases, Table & Calculators by Subject," U.S. Bureau of Labor Statistics, accessed March 11, 2022, https://data.bls.gov/timeseries/CUUR0000SA0?amp% 253bdata_tool=XGtable&output_view=data&include_graphs=true.

---

16   "Databases, Table & Calculators by Subject," U.S. Bureau of Labor Statistics, accessed March 11, 2022, https://data.bls.gov/timeseries/CUUR0000SA0?amp% 253bdata_tool=XGtable&output_view=data&include_graphs=true.

You may notice that three of a retiree's four largest expenditures have higher inflation rates compared to the average. Because these categories make up 72% of a retiree's expenditures, inflation is simply higher for a retiree compared to a pre-retiree. Based on their spending habits, a retiree's historical inflation rate is ~2.7%. At that rate, buying power greatly reduces over time. Though 2.7% doesn't sound like a high number, inflation may make an impact on a retiree's ability to save over time. After 10 years, a million dollars is only worth $781,656, and after 25 years, a million dollars is worth almost half as much. Table 8 outlines the impact of a 2.7% inflation rate on cash over time.

Table 8. *Impact of Inflation on Cash Value Over a 30-Year Period*

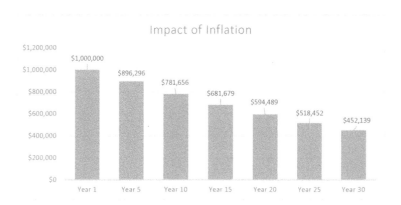

Source: Author, Derek Mazzarella, CFP.

While historically 2.7% is a fairly low inflation rate, what would happen if the recent inflation numbers of 2022, which reached a high of 9.1%,[17] lingered or we went back to the

---

17 U.S. Bureau of Labor Statistics, *Consumer Price Index—December 2022* [News Release USDL-23-0017], December 1, 2022, https://www.bls.gov/news.release/pdf/cpi.pdf.

higher inflation environment we had back in the '70s and '80s? To maintain your lifestyle, you'd have to increase your withdrawal rate each year by the inflation rate. The higher the inflation number, the worse it may get for a retiree. Table 9 shows how higher inflation rates may potentially affect your retirement based on three inflation rate scenarios.

Table 9. *Impact of Inflation While Making Withdrawals*

Impact of Inflation

Legend: 2.7% Inflation, 4.5% Inflation, 6% Inflation

Source: Author, Derek Mazzarella, CFP.

In all three scenarios, a retiree started with one million dollars invested in a 60/40 portfolio, withdrew $40,000 a year, and adjusted the withdrawals annually by the inflation rate. At 2.7%, that retiree would still end up with over a million dollars. They'd have $511,000 left with a 4.5% inflation rate and would run out of money by 2021 with a 6% inflation rate. By year 10, their $40,000 withdrawal becomes $50,839 (2.7%), $59,444 (4.5%), and $67,549 (6%).

Though a 6% inflation rate is unlikely to stay that high over a 20- or 30-year span, even spikes in the inflation rate for a few years may impact the overall health of your retirement. Inflation puts excess pressure on your assets to perform well in retirement. Combine high inflation with low return market returns, and you may be in serious financial trouble.

Inflation is a slow and steady risk for retirees. It often occurs in the background, goes unnoticed, and gets worse over time. Retirees should know that inflation is different for them compared to pre-retirees. Eventually, a retiree's bag of chips becomes more air than chip. How are your assets positioned to combat the impacts of inflation?

Chapter Highlights

- Inflation is a risk that reduces your buying power over time. What once cost $10 will later cost $15.
- Though the average inflation rate over the last 30 years has been 2.4%, it is 2.7% for a retiree.
- A retiree's spending habits differ from a pre-retiree's, so inflation rates affect them differently.
- Some of the most common retiree expenditures have higher inflation rates, such as healthcare, housing, food and beverage, and transportation.
- Ten years' worth of inflation may reduce buying power by almost 25%.
- Inflation may fluctuate over time, and periods of high inflation have happened before in the late '70s and early '80s.
- In 2022, inflation hit a high of 9.1%, and it may take a while for inflation to get back to pre-COVID-19 levels.

CHAPTER 7

TAXES—CAN I HAVE A BITE OF THAT?

At the time of writing this book, I have a three-year-old. He's great, but my wife and I can no longer snack in peace. I swear he has some sort of radar. If he hears a crinkling wrapper, he instantly slides right up next to me and asks, "What are you eating, Daddy?" Next thing I know, he's happily walking away with a part of my snack (or most of it). You know who else is like that? The government. But they aren't nearly as cute.

Whether you like it or not, the government is deeply involved in your retirement. Taxes don't go away once you're retired, and your retirement tax bracket may not even be lower than it is now. Most people assume that healthcare will be their number one expense; however, for many people, taxes are the largest expense in retirement. The IRS will come after you like a hungry child looking for a snack.

The Center for Retirement Research at Boston College reports that the average retiree pays about 6% of their income in federal and state income taxes,[18] but averages may be mis-

---

[18] Anqi Chen and Alicia H. Munnell, "How Much Taxes Will Retirees Owe on Their Income?" *Center for Retirement Research at Boston College*, no. 20-16

leading. Generally, people will fall into two categories: people in low tax brackets who should strategize how to stay there and retirees with higher incomes who are looking for avenues to reduce their tax bills. Higher-income earners, defined as a married couple that receives a combined $50,900 from social security and has 401(k)/IRA balances of $325,000 or more, pay an average of 11.3% of their income on taxes in retirement. If you're single and hitting those numbers, congrats, you have the financial strength of two people. If your goal is to have a successful and fulfilling retirement, odds are you'll fall into this category.

When it comes to taxes in retirement, there are three items you should be aware of: where tax rates could be in retirement, how social security is taxed, and how people currently plan for taxes in retirement.

WHERE WILL TAXES BE?

What was the highest marginal tax bracket in the history of the United States? Would you believe me if I said 75%? How about 85%? Too high? Actually, the highest marginal tax rate in the history of the United States was 94%. That was in 1944 and 1945 when we had a war to pay for and needed some dough. Today, the top marginal tax rate is 37%, which is set to increase in 2026 (unless Congress makes changes before then). Table 10 illustrates the history of tax rates.

(January 2021), https://crr.bc.edu/wp-content/uploads/2020/12/IB_20-16_.pdf.

Table 10. *Historical Top Marginal Tax Rates*

Source: JPMorgan Asset Management, *Guide to Retirement*[SM]: *2021 Edition*, accessed February 6, 2023, https://static.fmgsuite.com/media/documents/84196549-a3f6-4aa0-bfc4-a11d00a6768a.pdf.

As you can see, tax rates have been historically much higher than they've been today. If you consider our country's massive debt and historically low tax environment, where would you expect taxes to be in the future? Would you expect them to be higher or lower? My guess would be higher, but who really knows for sure. I'm fairly confident that tax rates won't get lower.

One other item to keep in mind is state tax rates. Location may play a significant role in retirement tax planning. In the United States, 41 of the 50 states have a state income tax, and some states have income tax rates over 10%. If you're a high-income earner, you could potentially pay 50% or more in taxes depending on the state you live in (when you combine federal and state taxes).

SOCIAL SECURITY

Social security income does not always come tax free. Depending on your combined income or provisional income, you may pay taxes on 0, 50, or 85% of your social security benefit. Table 11 outlines the 2022 combined income levels.

Table 11. *Social Security Taxable Income Thresholds*

Combined Income Amounts		Then
Married Filing Jointly	Other Taxpayers*	
$32,000 or less	$25,000 or less	Social security was tax free
Ranging From $32,000 to $44,000	Ranging From $25,000 to $34,000	Up to 50% of social security income was taxable
More than $44,000	More than $34,000	Up to 85% of social security income was taxable

Source: "Income Taxes and Your Social Security Benefit," Social Security Administration, accessed February 6, 2023, https://www.ssa.gov/benefits/retirement/planner/taxes.html.

*If you're married, filing separately, and do not live apart from your spouse at all times during the taxable year, up to 85% of your social security is taxable.

Note: Check out the website www.justretirealready.com for updated tax brackets.

As you may see from the table, if you're married and make less than $32,000, or if you aren't married and make less than $25,000, your social security payments will be fully tax free. Depending on your *combined income* amount, 50 or 85% of your benefit could be deemed taxable income, but that doesn't mean your tax rate is 50 or 85%.

What is *combined income*, and why did I italicize the term? Social security uses your combined income to determine your income brackets. Combined income may be represented as an equation:

$$\text{Your adjusted gross income} + \text{nontaxable interest} + \tfrac{1}{2} \text{ of your social security benefit} = \text{your combined income}$$

Breaking it down, your adjusted gross income consists of the following:

- Gross income, including wages
- Dividends
- Capital gains
- Business income
- Retirement distributions
- "Other income"

Your nontaxable income is income received that is not taxed but must be included on your tax return:

- Inheritances and gifts
- Cash rebates from a manufacturer
- Alimony
- Child support
- Most healthcare benefits
- Welfare payments
- **Municipal bond interest**

I highlighted municipal bond interest because most people assume that since they don't pay federal taxes on the interest, it wouldn't be included in the social security calculation, but they wouldn't be correct. Even with conventional tax planning, you may still subject your social security payments to income taxes.

HOW PEOPLE PLAN FOR TAXES IN RETIREMENT

Planning for taxes in retirement is where things get dicey. Lincoln Financial Group conducted a study on people between the ages of 62 and 75 who had incomes over $100,000, asking them what their primary tactic was to reduce their taxes.[19] Guess what the top answer was? Almost a quarter of respondents stated that *doing nothing* was their top strategy. Retirees have the same tax planning strategy as Austin Powers at the blackjack table: "I'll stay." The next most common response was to itemize deductions, but that does little to reduce taxes for most retirees.

One other challenge people face with taxes in retirement is how they treat taxes *before* retirement. An accountant's main goal is to save their clients as much as they may on their latest tax returns. Most people are constantly taught to reduce their taxes now. They save into pre-tax accounts to reduce their taxable income, and they save any extra into investment accounts. With that tactic, however, they've built up a significant tax time bomb by the time they get to retirement. At that point, conventional wisdom says to defer the taxes as long as possible; take income from your least tax-efficient accounts (taxable investment accounts), then take distributions from your deferred tax accounts. While this strategy may greatly reduce taxes early on in retirement, it creates an ever-increasing

---

[19] "The Underrated Impact of Taxes on Retirement," Lincoln Financial Group, accessed March 15, 2022, https://www.lfg.com/wcs-static/pdf/68%20percent%20The%20underrated%20impact%20of%20taxes%20on%20retireme.pdf.

tax obligation later. You're essentially kicking the tax can down the road for years.

All these tax delays create what is financially known as the "tax torpedo." When you reach a certain age, the IRS wants their money. They've waited long enough and are getting antsy. They require you to take money from your qualified accounts (accounts that have not yet been taxed, such as your traditional IRA or traditional 401(k)/403(b), even if you don't need the income. These are called your required minimum distributions (RMDs). RMDs increase your tax rate and tax liability because all distributions from a tax deferred account are taxed. RMDs may potentially increase your tax liability on your social security payments (if you're not already getting taxed on them), may move you up a tax bracket, and may possibly increase the cost of your Medicare Part B payments. These heavy tax implications create the tax torpedo. The conventional strategy may save you taxes now and early on in retirement, but you may end up paying more taxes throughout your retirement.

Sometimes when I go to the grocery store I have a shopping list, and sometimes I don't. If you're anything like me, when I have a list I tend to stick to it. When I don't have a shopping list, I tend to meander around more, buy on impulse (a.k.a. junk food), spend more money, and still want to go out to eat. Tax planning in retirement works the same way as having a shopping list. Going into retirement with a tax strategy may help you reduce your taxes, allowing you to enjoy more of your retirement.

Too often, people are reactionary with their tax planning and end up paying more in taxes in the long run. What is your tax strategy for retirement? What are you doing to minimize taxes over the life of your retirement?

Chapter Highlights

- Taxes will most likely be one of your largest expenses in retirement.
- Almost a quarter of retirees have no strategy to reduce taxes.
- Taxes today are historically low, and they will most likely be higher in the future.
- Social security is taxed depending on your provisional and/or combined income, which may include assets that generate tax-free income (such as municipal bonds).
- Deferring taxes in retirement may help minimize your tax bill early in retirement, but it may mean paying more taxes throughout your retirement.
- Required minimum distributions (RMDs) may increase both the cost of Medicare Part B premiums and the likelihood that your social security income will be taxed.

CHAPTER 8

LONGEVITY—OH, YOU'RE STILL HERE . . .

About to host a party, you've collected all the RSVPs and ordered catering from your favorite restaurant. The food was expensive, so you tried to order the right amount for everyone plus a little extra. As your party rolls on, you notice increasingly more people are showing up than you thought, plenty of whom didn't RSVP (how dare they?). As you count the numbers in your head, you start to panic because you're now realizing that you didn't order enough food. It's too late to order more, and now you need to make sure people don't take too much or your guests will go hungry. Everybody gets one meatball only!

Living longer than expected is like having more people come to a party than anticipated. You have a finite amount of money and expect it to last a certain amount of time. Most retirees consistently underestimate the length of their retirement. In fact, two-thirds of men and just over half of women underestimate their life expectancy (see table 12). When I work with clients, I project their retirement lasting to at least age 90. Most clients will tell me I'm crazy and they will never make it that long. Take a guess: How long would a current 65-year-old expect to live?

Table 12. *Probable Life Expectancy*

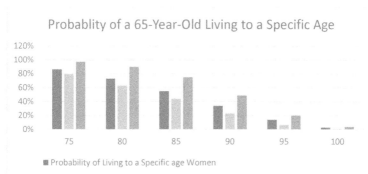

Probablity of a 65-Year-Old Living to a Specific Age

- ■ Probability of Living to a Specific age Women
- ▨ Probability of Living to a Specific age Men
- ■ Probability of Living to a Specific age Couple (at least one lives to a specific age)

Source: "Underestimating Years in Retirement," Stanford Center on Longevity, accessed March 14, 2022, https://longevity.stanford.edu/underestimating-years-in-retirement/.

A 65-year-old today could expect to live to their mid-80s and has a pretty good chance of living into their 90s. As medical advances continue, people should expect to live longer in the future. Couples tend to have a higher life expectancy compared to non-couples, and there's a nearly 50% chance that one person will live to age 90. So the next time your spouse gets mad at you for not vacuuming, just tell them you're helping them live longer. Argument over. (I know you didn't come here for marriage advice, but you're welcome.)

How does living longer relate to retirement planning? Of all the risks I mentioned so far, longevity risk may be the worst. Longevity risk is a retirement risk multiplier. The longer you live, the more stock market crashes you'll experience, the greater the stress of sequence of returns will be, the higher the risk of a healthcare event and subsequent costs, the more tax changes you'll be subject to, and the more impactful inflation will be. By 2050, if the average life expectancy has risen by three years, the cost of aging would increase 50%.[20] Ultimately, underestimating longevity risk may lead to a retiree's greatest fear: running out of money.

Figures 4 through 6 illustrate three sample retirement scenarios (Monte Carlo simulations) projecting the potential success rate of a retiree who passes away at either 80, 85, or 90.[21] In this context, a high potential success rate means a retiree won't run out of money while they continue spending it on what they want.

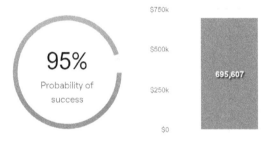

Figure 4: Projected Potential Success Rate for a Retiree Who Passes Away at Age 80

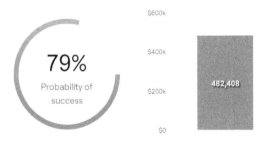

Figure 5: Projected Potential Success Rate for a Retiree Who Passes Away at Age 85

---

20   Stanford Center on Longevity, "Underestimating Years in Retirement."
21   Figures generated using RightCapital Financial Planning Software.

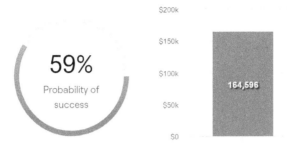

Figure 6: Projected Potential Success Rate for a Retiree Who Passes Away at Age 90

You may clearly see the impact of living five or 10 years longer in retirement. A retiree who lives to age 80 has a very high probability of success. If that same retiree lived to age 85, their potential success rate would drop to 79%, which is typically lower than we'd like to see but still doable with some adjustments. If the retiree lives to age 90, they have a far lower potential success rate of 59%. With that type of potential success rate, the retiree would need the market to do really well or may have to make more meaningful adjustments to their spending habits. Ten years doesn't sound like a long time, but people are living longer, and living to age 90 or older isn't out of the realm of possibilities.

Living longer puts more stress on your assets to outpace inflation, and it increases the likelihood of an additional market correction. It also means higher medical costs later in life and paying more taxes over time. Longevity makes all the other risks more prevalent.

You may look at stats all day and try to guess how long you'll live for. You may make it to age 67, or you may live to age 100. You won't ever know for sure, but you need to build a plan that's flexible enough to ensure you may enjoy your life both early on and later in retirement in case you're lucky enough to live a long life. The only way to deal with longevity now is to spend less as you age. You need to make sure you have enough meatballs for everyone. What plan do you have in place to ensure you don't run out of money?

Chapter Highlights

- Retirees consistently underestimate their life expectancy.
- A 65-year-old may expect to live to their mid-80s.
- Couples tend to have a higher life expectancy compared to non-couples, and there's a high chance that at least one person will live to age 90.
- Retirement potential success rates decrease exponentially the longer you live.
- Longevity risk is a risk multiplier that may compound all other risks.
- Longevity increases the odds that you'll run out of money in retirement.

CHAPTER 9

I'M GOING FIRST

You see this issue with athletes all the time: They suffer an injury but try to keep playing. To keep playing, their body must compensate for the injury by putting excess stress on other parts of the body. What started out as a foot injury on one leg becomes a knee injury on the other. The extra stress is subtle, but it builds over time and creates a worse outcome. Couples in retirement may have scenarios that play out like this.

My wife always tells me that we have to die at the same time, like in the ending of *The Notebook*. As much as I love the thought of that, it isn't realistic; couples usually don't die on the same day. Losing the love of your life, the person you shared your life with, is challenging enough. The harsh reality is that one of you will likely die first, and I want to make sure both of you are financially prepared for that scenario.

Let's use an example to show how one spouse's retirement income will be affected by the death of the other. Currently, Sam is collecting $24,000 a year from social security, and Pat is collecting $30,000 a year. As a couple, they need $100,000 of income each year in retirement, so they take the remaining $46,000 from their traditional 401(k) plan (all distributions are taxed). They are both 70 years old, which means they have to start taking out their RMDs soon.

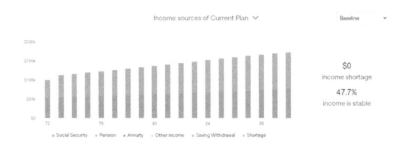

Figure 7: Income Sources for Sam and Pat's Retirement. Figure generated using RightCapital Financial Planning Software.

As figure 7 indicates, their plan looks good overall. They have an 83% probability of having a successful retirement if they both live to age 90. But what would happen if Pat were to pass away at age 75?

- Sam would lose one of their social security payments but would be able to collect the highest one. Meaning, Sam would be able to keep collecting Pat's $30,000 social security benefit but would lose his $24,000 benefit.
- Sam would still have to take out RMDs based on his age/mortality table.
- Sam would have to replace his $24,000 of social security income with fully taxable 401(k) distributions.
- Sam would have a higher tax rate and pay more taxes.
- Sam's probability of success would drop to 77%.

Figure 8 shows what this would look like for Sam.

Figure 8: Sam's Income Sources in Retirement after Pat's Death. Figure generated using RightCapital Financial Planning Software.

As you may tell from the figure, Sam's stable income (social security) drops, he's more reliant on 401(k) distributions, and his taxes increase.

In addition, Sam's federal tax rate increases from just over 10 to 16.5%, and he ends up paying about $59,610 more in taxes over the course of his retirement. Sam's taxes increased for three reasons:

1. Whereas traditional 401(k) distributions are fully taxable, only 85% of social security income is taxable in Sam's case. Since more of Sam's income now comes from 401(k) distributions rather than social security, dollar for dollar more of Sam's retirement income is taxable.
2. Sam must keep the same RMD schedule.
3. Sam's tax filing status changed from married filing jointly to single, which lowers the income tax threshold brackets.

Three main ripple effects occur when one spouse dies before the other during retirement: reduction of social security income, increased taxes due to changing sources of income, and more pressure put on market-based assets to generate income. RMDs will see little change since they will pass over to the surviving spouse's RMD schedule (this would be different if the spouses had a larger age gap).

Maybe things will work out and you and your spouse will die together like in the movies. If that doesn't happen, though, you need to understand the financial implications of your spouse's death on your retirement. The loss of social security income and increased tax liability puts extra stress on your retirement portfolio to perform. How may you best prepare for the worst?

Chapter Highlights

- Most couples plan their retirement assuming they will pass away at relatively the same time.
- When one spouse passes, the surviving spouse loses one source of social security income.
- The surviving spouse's income is subject to more market risk since they need to replace the income from social security.
- The surviving spouse's tax rates increase most often because their tax bracket thresholds are lower and they need to take more income from their savings, which is usually taxed.
- Required minimum distributions (RMDs) may not change much if spouses are close in age.
- If you're married, it's best practice to evaluate what would happen should one of you die earlier than expected.

CHAPTER 10

DID WE JUST SWING AND MISS?

W ell, that was a lot. How pumped are you to retire now? Retirees will deal with market risk, sequence of returns risk, inflation, taxes, longevity, and even early death. You may be thinking, *So let me get this straight. You can die too early and live too long? How does anyone actually retire when so much may go wrong?*

As you reflect on the retirement challenges mentioned in the previous chapters, it may be helpful to take a beat and assess how resilient your retirement is to each retirement risk. Here are some assessment questions to get you thinking about how you're currently set up to handle them.

- **Market Risk:** How is your portfolio set up for or how will it change in retirement? How would you react if your portfolio lost 15–20% or more?
- **Sequence of Returns Risk:** How would your portfolio handle a market loss in the first few years either before or after you retire? Would your portfolio be able to generate the income you'd need to live on, and would it last for the rest of your life?

- **Healthcare:** What is your plan to minimize healthcare costs in retirement? What are you doing to keep your Medicare premiums low? How would you handle a significant long-term care event?
- **Taxes:** Other than itemizing, what are you doing to reduce you tax bill in retirement? Have you looked at what tax bracket you'll fall under in retirement?
- **Longevity:** What are you doing to ensure that your money lasts throughout your retirement? What is your backup plan in case you do live longer than you think?
- **Death of a Spouse:** Have you factored in how your income would change if one of you were to die before the other? How would your social security payments change? Would your assets be able to create enough income to cover that gap?

I encourage you to really think about answering each question. Take some time to think them through and write down your answers. As you're writing, reflect on which answers you feel confident in and which questions are giving you pause. These retirement risks are real, but they aren't insurmountable.

Please, don't feel stressed if you don't know all the answers. As I've mentioned, most of us aren't very good at retiring. In most cases, using traditional planning strategies may not be enough to combat the retirement risks we've discussed. We can't rely on the traditional way of thinking about retirement anymore. Retirement puts more pressure on you now than in the past. We simply haven't been given enough of the tools needed to deal with all the retirement challenges that come our way.

In baseball scouting, there's a term that describes an incredibly talented player. If a scout calls a player a "five-tool prospect," that means the player may do everything on the baseball field at an elite level. They may run fast, hit for power and average, play great defense, and have a cannon for an arm. Most people go into retirement with only two tools: their retirement portfolio (stocks and bonds) and social security. They may hit and run, but they're constantly dropping the ball in the outfield.

I want you to be prepared for any financial event or retirement risk at an elite level. Retirement should be as worry free as possible. When you don't have a financial game plan, retirement risks may add a level of underlying anxiety. So let's give your retirement "five-tool prospect" status.

In this and the upcoming chapters, I'm going to discuss the different financial tools available to you and break down how they may potentially help you reduce certain retirement risks. I'll outline a financial tool, the types of risk it helps you avoid, and some of its potential faults. Not every financial tool and strategy will be a fit for you and your situation, but I encourage you to have an open mind about them. My aim is to educate you on the solutions that are available. Some of these strategies will be familiar to you and some may not be. Some tools will help you reduce one or more retirement risks, and you may find that you won't need to implement all the strategies since some may provide overlapping benefits. Some strategies may not be available to everyone. Consider these tools as vehicles for helping you generate the most amount of income in retirement.

As you read about each of the upcoming tools, think about how you answered your assessment questions, how you could implement the tool, if it would cover a gap you feel you have, and whether it would reduce some of your financial stress. This whole process is about finding out which tools would be the right fit for *you* so you may have the retirement *you* want.

CHAPTER 11

IT'S LIKE A BUFFET BUT WITH INVESTMENTS

Retirement Tool: Portfolio Diversification
Retirement Risks: Market, Sequence of Returns

When it comes to investing, I want you to think of ice cream. Picture yourself owning an ice cream store. Would you sell one flavor of ice cream? Having different flavors of ice cream will help cater to people's different tastes. Would you sell more ice cream in the winter or the summer? If you decided to add hot chocolate, you'd have another product to sell in the winter to help balance out the drop in ice cream sales. An ice cream shop with a variety of flavors and products helps provide balance. A diverse portfolio works the same way.

Diversification is probably the most overused term in financial planning and investing, but there's a reason for that. With investing comes risk—risks that are somewhat under your control and risks that aren't. The two overarching types of risk are known as "systematic risk" and "unsystematic" risk. Systematic risk refers to overall market risks, which unfortunately you have little control over. You can't control overall market performance, interest-rate changes, global conflicts, or what a president tweets. Systematic risk is like the tide; it affects all the boats in the ocean, and the size or type of your boat doesn't necessarily matter. Unsystematic risk is more in your control. It involves evaluating risks with individual companies, sectors, and/or asset classes.

Investing all your money in a single company or a particular sector (such as technology or energy) may be risky. From 2017 to 2021, 33% of US individual stocks lost money. By comparison, just 0.1% of mutual funds and exchange-traded funds lost money during the same time frame.[22] We aren't even talking about investing in a small company like Fred's Bug Control. These are massive publicly traded companies. Trying to pick a company or a few companies to invest in doesn't make sense for a retiree. It's too risky.

Building a portfolio is like putting a band together. If you had a band made up entirely of drummers, even if they were the best drummers in the world, you probably wouldn't have a lot of people listening to your music. If you had a band of all lead guitarists, they would constantly play over each other and you'd end up with mostly noise. The best bands have a mix of instruments and the right balance, and each band member brings something different in a way that complements the rest.

Within an investment portfolio, asset classes act in a similar way. Each type of asset has a role to play and adds to the performance of your portfolio. Some assets are for safety, some are for income, and some are for growth. Some will work better in down markets, while others will work better in up markets. Asset classes perform differently depending on the type of market you're in. Having a blend of assets in your portfolio most

---

[22] Dennis Lee, "When the Outlook is Blurry, Put on an After-Tax Lens," BlackRock Advisor Center, May 18, 2022, https://www.blackrock.com/us/financial-professionals/insights/after-tax.

likely means that you'll never outpace the market, but it will help prevent wild swings in the performance of your portfolio.

Investment portfolios come with their own risks, and I've seen a few common mistakes with them over the years: overlap and/or concentration with investments, lack of cohesion between different account types, and those that are misaligned with the portfolio's time frame. Portfolio overlap occurs when many of the same funds own the same stock or bond. You may have a portfolio with several mutual funds or exchange-traded funds, but each of those funds may be investing in the same company stock. It's like a house that's been renovated but has a toilet in the bathroom and the kitchen.

Many people have different account types, including a 401(k), a Roth IRA, and an investment account. They'll typically invest in each account differently, with little or no thought about how each of the accounts are related to each other. These accounts are often invested in silos. It's helpful to determine which account you'd withdraw from first, know what each of your accounts own, and recognize how they fit with each other. This is where portfolio diversification comes in.

Diversification doesn't mean just buying different types of assets. If you were going to cook something, you wouldn't buy pie crust, fish, and yogurt to make a meal. Those are different ingredients, but they *definitely* don't go together. Diversification means putting together assets in a cohesive manner. The goal of diversification is to reduce volatility and increase predictability of returns. Your retirement investment philosophy should center around creating the most return with the least amount of volatility or risk. You want to win by not losing. Diversification may help with that, even though it may feel like you're underperforming at times.

BlackRock Adviser Center put together a chart that sums up what it may feel like to invest with a diversified portfolio (see table 13). In looking back to 2000, you may notice there are three time frames when the S&P 500 was positive. Compared to a 60/40 portfolio, the S&P 500 outperformed in two of those time frames and did so by a good margin. However, there were also three negative return periods, and the diverse portfolio didn't lose nearly as much as the S&P 500 did. Ultimately, the returns were about the same over the time frame, but when you're retired and taking withdrawals, a portfolio with fewer losses is more important. Remember, stacking a more significant market loss with a portfolio withdrawal could put you in a larger financial hole than you're able to dig yourself out of.

Table 13. *Comparison of a Diversified Portfolio to the S&P 500 Index*

Years	S&P 500 Index	Diversified Portfolio
2000–2002	-40.1%	-15.7%
2003–2007	+82.9%	+87.1%
2008	-37.0%	-26.6%
2009–2019	+351.0%	+219.7%
Q1 2020	-30.4%	-23.1%
Q2 2020–2021	+119.0%	+66.6%
2022	-18.1%	-15.5%
Total Return Growth of $100,000	+288.6%	+301.6%
	$388,610	**$401,550**

Source: "Diversification May Feel Disappointing," BlackRock Adviser Center, accessed September 16, 2022, https://www.blackrock.com/us/individual/literature/investor-education/diversification-may-feel-disappointing-sp-envy-va-us.pdf.

So how do you go about building better diversified investment portfolios? There are many aspects to building one, but the two main items to keep in mind when it comes to diversification are volatility and correlation.

VOLATILITY

Think of a seesaw with one person on each end. That seesaw will swing all the way up and all the way down. But if you add more people to both sides of the seesaw, there won't be as many wild swings. When it comes to investing, portfolios work the same way; with only one or a few investments, retirees may experience wild swings and more volatility. Well-diversified portfolios could have more balance and may experience less volatility.

Portfolio volatility is a measurement of the range of returns you may reasonably expect to experience with an investment. One of the key measures of volatility is standard deviation. The higher the standard deviation of an asset or portfolio, the greater the volatility. For example, let's say there are two portfolios, each with an average return of 5% per year. Portfolio A has a standard deviation of 10, while portfolio B has a standard deviation of 15. With 95% of returns falling within two standard deviations, portfolio B will have a wider range of returns. In this situation, portfolio A's range of returns will be -15 to 25%, and portfolio B's range of returns will be between -25 and 35%. A retiree's goal is to try to build a portfolio with adequate returns while seeking to minimize risk.

CORRELATION

Correlation within a portfolio relates to how different asset classes move in relation to each other. Do they move together or separately? Using the ice cream store analogy, ice cream sales will do better in the summer, and sales will move in the same direction regardless of whether you have 10 flavors or 25. Hot chocolate, on the other hand, will sell better in the winter, so hot chocolate sales will not move in the same direction as ice cream sales. They are considered non-correlated.

Generally, bonds will be up when stocks are down, although there have been some exceptions. Alternative investments, such as in commodities or natural resources, will move separately from both stocks and bonds. Correlations work on a scale from 1.0, which is perfectly correlated, to -1.0. A score of zero means the assets are non-correlated, so they move independently. Correlations also change over time.

A well-diversified portfolio contains a mix of assets that may not react the same way in different types of markets. The benefit of mixing negatively correlated assets into a portfolio is a potential reduction in volatility. When one asset class is doing well, the other may have a negative return, or vice versa. Overall, having a properly correlated portfolio can provide balance in a variety of market conditions.

To recap, having exposure to various asset classes that don't move in the same direction as other assets will help reduce your investment risk. To provide balance, you want to have different varieties of ice cream and hot chocolate. When you become a retiree, your best course of action is to seek to have a more stable and consistently performing portfolio, even if that means giving up some upside. Your individual portfolio should consistently line up with your individual risks and timelines.

Chapter Highlights

- There are two types of risk: systematic and unsystematic. Systematic risk is overall market risk, and unsystematic is company-level risk.
- Portfolio diversification involves building a portfolio of asset classes that move in separate directions in different types of markets.

- Diversification seeks to reduce overall portfolio risk and volatility.
- Diversification usually means rarely coming in first, but it means not coming in last, either.

CHAPTER 12

GRAB A BUCKET

Retirement Tool: The Bucket Strategy
Retirement Risks: Market, Sequence of Returns, Inflation

Traditionally, when investors get to retirement, they reduce the number of stocks they own and buy more bonds. While a retiree should own fewer equities (stocks) compared to a 30-year-old, it's hard to know exactly how much. There's an old adage that says a person should own their age in bonds: a 25-year-old's portfolio would hold 25% in bonds, and a 65-year-old's portfolio would hold 65%. This is dumb advice, so please ignore it. For most people, having their age in bonds would mean their portfolio is too conservative and will lose out on the excess returns the stock market may provide.

Retirees have a few challenges when it comes to picking their mix of stocks and bonds. If a retiree is too conservative, their portfolio may not keep up with their spending or inflation and they may run out of money. If a retiree is too aggressive, they may not be able to recover from a market correction—or three. A 50/50 (stocks/bonds) or 60/40 portfolio is the traditional allocation suggestion for retirees. Investing your retirement funds with the same allocation can mean you're taking income from the proportionate number of stocks and bonds. A fixed allocation portfolio is somewhat rigid, and it may not protect you from a market drop as much as you'd think, especially when stocks and bonds are down in the same year which we saw in 2022.

We aren't robots, so emotion does play a role in how we invest. Staying invested in down markets is a significant challenge for retirees. When you have only a finite amount of money, you feel your losses much more significantly. We can't eliminate emotion, but we may reduce emotional overreaction. That brings us to the bucket strategy, which means breaking your retirement assets into three time-based buckets: immediate, mid-term, and long-term.

IMMEDIATE BUCKET

The immediate bucket's job is to keep your retirement funds nice and safeguarded, like a child clutching their blankie during a thunderstorm. The stock market may crash multiple times during your retirement. Having an immediate bucket of cash available can help insulate you from those market crashes, giving you the confidence of knowing you're going to be OK and don't need to overreact.

The first step in the bucket strategy is to determine your annual retirement expenses. You should split your expenses into two categories: fixed and variable. Fixed expenses are those that are consistent on a monthly basis, such as rent or mortgage, Medicare payments, cell phone bills, and groceries. Variable expenses are those that continually change, such as paying for entertainment, going out to eat, spoiling the grandkids, or enjoying the general fun items in life. Since they are dependable and predictable, fixed expenses should be covered by consistent income sources, such as social security, a pension, or annuities. The bucket strategy is designed to cover the variable expenses in your retirement.

An immediate bucket should consist of two years' worth of retirement expenses. The funds in your immediate bucket should be kept in liquid cash-based savings accounts. If you want to get crazy, feel free to put the second years' worth of expenses in short duration bonds. Keeping two years' worth of cash available is designed to help you reduce the urge to make any drastic changes with your investment portfolio. A 20% drop in the market will typically take between one to two years to recover from. Having the funds in cash will help give you the ability to weather a down market.

Quick Tip: Keeping three months' worth of cash available in your emergency fund can prevent you from withdrawing too much cash in case there's an emergency and a down market at the same time.

MID-TERM BUCKET

The mid-term bucket's job is to generate some return and create a source of income. The mid-term bucket is like a Volvo; rather than being a fancy fast car, it's meant to be safe and reliable. The focus here is quality and income.

A mid-term bucket will cover at least three to five years' worth of expenses (if you're conservative, you may extend this by a year or two). The overall allocation should be 30 to 40% in stocks, with the rest in high-quality bonds (depending on interest rates). If interest rates are low, you may need to increase your equity exposure. The equity piece of your portfolio should favor quality stocks and/or equities that produce dividends and/or income. If your portfolio produces enough income, you may use that to refill your immediate bucket. If the funds themselves don't produce enough income, you may need to sell gains to fill the gap.

LONG-TERM BUCKET

The job of the long-term bucket is to generate higher returns. With this bucket, you need to put the pedal to, or close to, the metal. Inflation is a looming risk in retirement, and if your portfolio is too conservative, it may not be able to generate enough return to handle your withdrawal demand and the negative effects of inflation.

A long-term bucket consists of your remaining retirement assets. Funds in the long-term bucket should be equity-heavy, usually 70 to 80% stocks. The stocks in your portfolio should be those that grow naturally, and the bonds may be higher risk, such as high yield bonds. Of the three bucket strategies, a long-term bucket may have the most variability. Refer to figure 9 for an illustrative outline of how to segment your three retirement buckets.

Short-Term Bucket   **Mid-Term Bucket**   **Long-Term Bucket**

2 Years of Expenses   3-5 Years of Expenses   6+ Years of Expenses

Figure 9: Bucket Strategy Outline

MANAGING THE BUCKET STRATEGY

It's important to periodically rebalance your portfolio, which involves resetting it back to its intended equity-to-bond ratio. For example, if stocks have a good year, your original 80/20 (stocks/bonds) allocation may change to 85/15. Rebalancing would involve selling the 5% in excess stocks and buying bonds to reset your allocation back to 80/20. This would help ensure that you're selling gains and buying underperforming positions.

As you might be noticing, the bucket strategy is more dynamic compared to a traditional portfolio, which is one of its positive features. However, the extra supervision needed may be a negative. Here's a breakdown of how to best manage the buckets:

- Each year, evaluate your portfolio and move money from your long-term bucket to your mid-term bucket, and from your mid-term bucket to your immediate bucket. This will refill your cash position.
- Depending on your cash flow and the performance of the stock market, you don't always need exactly two years' worth of cash in your immediate bucket. You have the option to be flexible here. For example, in a down market, you may want to stop shifting from your mid- and long-term buckets to give your accounts time to recover.
- The income from your dividends and bond holdings should not be reinvested and should be swept into your immediate bucket.
- Set up rebalancing for your mid- and long-term buckets. It's best to automate this so that rebalancing occurs consistently. I recommend rebalancing quarterly or at least semiannually.
- Both your mid- and long-term buckets should consist of diversified portfolios.
- You'll have the most leeway with your long-term bucket, and this is the most important bucket to manage since it will be the most volatile. It's good practice to sell when the stock market is doing well and hold

when the stock market is performing poorly. A general rule of thumb is to hold when there's a loss of 10% or more.

Realistically, you should have to adjust your portfolio only a few times a year. At the end of the year, you'll want to reassess the past year's spending rate to gain an idea of your cash needs for the upcoming year and make the appropriate changes. Establishing a bucket strategy will help you avoid the emotional pitfalls of investing since your portfolio would be set up to weather market downturns.

Chapter Highlights

- Most retirees have their funds in one overall allocation, which increases their overall market risk and sequence of returns risk.
- Bucketing your retirement funds into three separate time-based buckets may help insulate your portfolio from market risks and help it earn enough to combat inflation:
  1. Immediate bucket—two years' worth of variable expenses that are kept in a cash account. One year may be kept in a CD if you choose.
  2. Mid-term bucket—three to five years' worth of variable expenses that can be invested in 30 to 40% stocks, with the rest in bonds.
     - Stocks ideally should be made up of more established companies that pay dividends.
     - Bonds can more likely be short- or intermediate term and of higher quality.
  3. Long-term bucket—the remaining funds and the most aggressive investment bucket, made up of 70 to 80% stocks.

- Stocks in this bucket may be higher risk and higher growth.
- Bonds may be higher yield, lower quality, and longer duration.
- The bucket strategy should be managed at least once or twice a year. Funds should flow from your long-term bucket to your mid-term bucket to your immediate bucket.
- Remember to keep some flexibility based on the performance of the market.
- Go to the website www.justretirealready.com for a bucket strategy worksheet.

CHAPTER 13

I'M DANCING ON MY OWN

Retirement Tool: Permanent Life Insurance
Retirement Risks: Market, Sequence of Returns, Taxes

There are often debates in the financial world about this investment product or solution versus that investment product or solution, such as stocks versus bonds and index funds versus mutual funds. We make a mistake in saying "or" when we should be saying "and." The question shouldn't be this *or* that, it should be how much of this do we integrate *with* that? What's the right mix?

Traditionally, retirees would invest in a mix of stocks and bonds, but even the most well-diversified portfolios have their limitations. While you may minimize market risk with a two-year cash reserve, there is a downside to doing so: holding too much cash may create a drag on your portfolio. A more stable retirement involves layering assets outside your financial portfolio, such as permanent life insurance.

If you Google "permanent life insurance," you may see a variety of negative comments ranging from "Brokers only sell it to collect high commissions" to "It's strictly a bad investment." Investments are like tools—if you try to use a hammer to cut down a tree, does that make the hammer a bad tool?

Investment tools are no different. When an investment tool is used for the wrong person in the wrong situation, then it's a bad investment. But when the investment tool is used correctly, it may be a great investment.

One challenge I see marketing these types of insurance products is how they are sold to people. They will say that life insurance is the most versatile investment there is and life insurance provides a death benefit, builds cash tax free, allows loans to be taken tax free, pays for itself in the event of a disability, and provides some long-term care benefits. Amazing! Who wouldn't want that? The problem here is that while life insurance *can* do all those things, it can't do them all at once. For example, if you withdraw cash or take a loan from your policy and never pay it back, your death benefit will be reduced.

It's important to have a plan when it comes to investing in permanent life insurance. Are you buying life insurance for the death benefit, or are you buying it to build up the cash value? The type of policy you invest in should line up with your financial goals. The point is, investing in a non-correlated asset (an asset that isn't tied to the performance of the stock market, such as permanent life insurance) may reduce the failure rate of your retirement plan when you have a focused strategy for the policy. Think of an non-correlated asset as a guy dancing to his own beat at a wedding. Everyone else is dancing to one beat, but this guy is over there doing his own thing and loving it. Having an asset that doesn't follow the normal beat of the market may provide balance.

There are four main types of permanent life insurance: universal, variable, indexed, and whole. Here's a quick outline of each of them:[23]

---

[23]   Check out the website www.justretirealready.com for a more comprehensive life insurance comparison.

1. **Universal**

   Universal life insurance builds cash value based on the interest-rate returns of your policy and are interest-rate sensitive. Universal policies will perform well in high interest-rate environments like we had in the '80s and worse in low-interest-rate environments like we had in the 2010s.

2. **Variable**

   With variable life insurance, cash value returns are based on the underlying performance of the mutual fund investments within a policy. Variable policies are the most volatile since their returns are tied to their underlying investment, and variable policy values may lose money.

3. **Indexed**

   In indexed life insurance, cash value returns are based on an index such as the S&P 500. These policies provide a floor so you can't lose money, but the upside is also capped. If the cap is 6%, for example, you're earning between 0% (if the return of the index is flat or negative) and 6% (if the index returns 6% or more).

4. **Whole Life**

   Whole life insurance builds cash value based on dividend payouts. These payouts are based on a combination of the life insurance company's revenue, investment returns, and ability to control their costs.

While variable policies have their pluses, they are too tied to the market or interest rates to be a fit for the strategies I'm about to explain. Whole life insurance returns aren't sexy, but that's the point. They have historical returns similar to bonds, but without the same risks (e.g., default, reinvestment, interest rate, and purchasing power). While bonds can be a safer investment compared to stocks, they may still lose value. Whole life insurance policies are contractually obligated to give you a positive return. In some cases, you may be able to replace a whole life policy with an indexed or universal one, but I'm going to focus on the most predictable permanent policy, whole life. In retirement, you may leverage a permanent life policy in several ways, each of which I describe next.

LEVERAGE THE DEATH BENEFIT

Retirement planning would be easy if we knew when we'll die. As a result, many people tend to be more conservative with how they spend in retirement. They typically take smaller withdrawals over the course of their retirement because they need to keep enough money available for future retirement years.

How can you leverage your death benefit to create more income in retirement? Wade Pfau and Michael Finke outline a concept in their white paper, "Integrating Whole Life Insurance into a Retirement Income Plan." In it, they pair a whole life policy with a single premium immediate annuity (SPIA).[24] It's 28 pages, feel free to read it, but if you're not a financial nerd like me, you may find it a bit technical. I'll save you the trouble and summarize how it works.

The first step is to purchase a whole life insurance policy. Then, when you're ready to take distributions in retirement,

---

[24] Wade D. Pfau and Michael Finke, "Integrating Whole Life Insurance into a Retirement Income Plan: Emphasis on Cash Value as a Volatility Buffer Asset," The American College of Financial Services, April 2019, https://retirementincomejournal.com/wp-content/uploads/2020/03/WBC-Whitepaper-Integrating-Whole-Life-Insurance-into-a-Retirement-Income-Plan-Emphasis-on-Cash-Value-as-a-Volatility-Buffer-Asset.pdf.

take from your investments the amount equal to your death benefit and invest that amount in an income annuity. For example, if you have a death benefit of $250,000, you would invest that full amount into an income-generating annuity such as an SPIA. You don't necessarily have to use an SPIA, but Pfau and Finke use one in their analysis. In return for an up-front sum of money or principal, SPIAs provide immediate income for the rest of your life.

There are three reasons this strategy may work:

1. Annuities may provide a larger income stream compared to a traditional withdrawal rate.
2. Income annuities are not subject to market risk or sequence of returns risk.
3. On a tax-free basis, the death benefit from a whole life policy is available to replace the funds that were invested into an annuity when a retiree passes away.

The biggest downside of an SPIA is that it has no death benefit. If you die, your family doesn't receive any of the money back, even if the insurance carrier provided you with just one payment. The death benefit from your life insurance policy covers this issue.

Table 14 illustrates this strategy, using the annuity rates as of the writing of this book and comparing them with the traditional safe withdrawal rate.

Table 14. *Traditional Withdrawal Rate Compared to an SPIA /*
Life Insurance Strategy

	Starting Amount	Payout Rate	Annual Income
Traditional "Safe" Withdrawal	$250,000	4.00%	$10,000
SPIA + Life Insurance	$250,000	7.45%*	$18,642

Source: Sample quotes generated using AIG's member SPIA calculator.

Note: *Rate as of January 5, 2023, based on a 65-year-old female.

Naturally, since premiums for a whole life policy are more expensive compared to term life insurance plans, you'll have fewer assets to withdraw from if you decide to invest in a whole life policy. As you may see from the table, using an annuity increases the annual income by more than $8,000, which in many cases is enough to offset the cost of the whole life policy. Your end goal should be to maximize income, not have the most assets.

Alternatively, you may use a universal life insurance policy with this strategy. Universal life insurance policies have lower premiums compared to whole life policies, but the cash value buildup isn't as valuable. Universal life policies may be designed to minimize the cash value and maximize the death benefit.

Universal life insurance policies tend to be riskier compared to whole life policies because they're more sensitive to interest rates. A long period of low interest rates may require you to add more premiums to a universal life policy if the policy isn't building enough cash value. You may reduce that risk by investing in a universal life insurance policy that provides a guaranteed death benefit to a certain age. If you're interested in exploring this strategy, I suggest running illustrations on both life insurance options to see whether one would be a better fit for you compared to the other.

Use the Cash Value for Income

You may access the cash value within a permanent life insurance policy through a withdrawal or a loan. You'll pay taxes on withdrawals for any amount greater than what you paid into the policy. Loans may be taken from the policy on a tax-free basis, and policy loans may be paid back directly by the insured or through the death benefit when a policy holder passes away. Using a life insurance policy's cash value for income may help improve your retirement outcomes in three ways: it may help you spend down more of your retirement assets since you have a supplemental income source, it may provide a source of tax-free income, and it may provide a stable, nonmarket-based income.

If you decide on this life insurance strategy, know that you're choosing the cash value over the death benefit. Taking loans out over time will diminish the death benefit available to your heirs when they are not paid back. Depending on your personal situation the best way to maximize this strategy is to overfund your life insurance policy. Each policy has a base premium and an option to overfund it that's called "paid up additions." Basically, you pay more into the policy than the required premiums. If the premium is $1,000, for example, you would send the carrier $2,000.

When you buy a life insurance policy, a portion of the premium goes toward paying for the insurance coverage. When you overfund the policy, a smaller portion of the excess premium goes toward increasing the death benefit, and a greater percentage of the premiums go toward building cash value. As a result, the returns on the excess premiums are typically greater than the base premiums. Overfunding your policy makes sense when you're looking to utilize your whole life policy for income. It's one of the only times in life when it makes sense to overpay for something.

Your situation may be different, but in running different scenarios I've found that taking consistent income over time is a better way to maximize the value of a life insurance policy compared to taking out chunks of money at different intervals. Table 15 depicts what this would look like for a 35-year-old male and a 50-year-old male, both having a preferred health rating (second-best), paying for premiums until age 65, then taking income every year until age 90.

Table 15. *Life Insurance Cash Value Projections for Two Scenarios*

Age	Annual Premium	Paid Up Additions (Additional Premium)	Cash Value @ Age 65	Annual Income	Total Income 25 Years
35	$3,805	$2,000	$334,981	$17,525	$438,125
50	$6,485	$3,000	$159,729	$7,260	$181,500

Note: Sample quotes generated using Guardian's Whole Life 99 life insurance illustrations at preferred rates; illustration 2021-121800, prepared by Derek Mazzarella, CFP.

As the table indicates, a 35-year-old would be able to generate $17,525 a year of tax-free income from their policy each year for 25 years, while a 50-year-old would be able to generate $7,260 a year for 25 years. You may have noticed that the younger you are, the better this strategy may work for you.

You may also look at these numbers and think you'd have more money if you just invested it in the stock market—the old "buy-term-and-invest-the-difference" crowd. You'd most likely be right since the stock market has more upsides. Yet there's also more risk involved in investing in the market. Because of market risk, you may have more money by retirement, but would you be able to generate as much income?

This blended strategy is meant to augment your investment in stocks and replace a *portion* of your bond portfolio. Table 16 shows how an integrated strategy may increase your income in retirement with less market risk.

Table 16. *Retirement Income Comparing Strategies*

Age & Strategy	Asset Value @ 65	After-Tax Income from Investments	Life Insurance Income	Total Combined Annual Income
35 Life + Investments	$439,754	$14,952	$17,525	$32,477
35 Investments Only	$881,877	$29,984	$0	$29,984
50 Life + Investments	$281,542	$9,572	$7,260	$16,832
50 Investments Only	$487,416	$16,572	$0	$16,752

Note: For these sample quotes, I assumed the 35-year-old started with $75,000 in an investment account and the 50-year-old started with $125,000. For the investment-only option, the premium was invested each year. There were no additional investments made in the life insurance plus investment option. The returns were based on the median outcome of J. P. Morgan's capital market assumptions using RightCapital's planning software. A 15% tax rate was used.

Looking at the table, you may see that both the 35-year-old and the 50-year-old have more assets with the investments-only strategy once they reach age 65 (I assumed the cost of the whole life premiums were invested in an after-tax investment account). Comparatively, a retirement income plan that integrates whole life insurance generates more income compared to a traditional withdrawal strategy and does so with less market risk. Would you rather have more assets or more income?

An integrated strategy has three main benefits compared to a traditional investment-only strategy. First, whole life insurance creates a source of stable income with less market risk because carriers are contractually obligated to generate a positive return for their policyholders. If you look back in history, an insurance carrier with a good financial rating has paid a dividend even in down markets. When most other asset classes lost money, life insurance carriers were paying out dividends to their policyholders.

Second, whole life policies are more tax efficient than an investment account. A permanent life insurance policy is tax sheltered during the growth phase, and loans may be taken from the policy tax free. If you have an investment account, you probably know the pain of receiving a 1099 every year that details the taxable income from the activity of your investment account, even when you never actually take out any money. After tax, those accounts will generate taxable gains under three scenarios: when dividends are received from investments (even if the dividends are reinvested), if a fund decides to sell an underlying position for a gain, and when taxable interest is earned (such as an interest payment from a bond). According to BlackRock Adviser Center, the average actively managed large-cap growth fund has a tax drag of 1.79% per year.[25] Even

---

[25]   Michael Lane, "Don't Let Taxes Drag You Down," BlackRock Adviser Center, May 26, 2021, https://www.blackrock.com/us/financial-professionals/insights/preparing-portfolios-for-taxes.

if you have a tax-efficient investment account, you'll still pay a capital gains tax on any growth when you sell the positions in the account. At a 15% tax rate, you would need to withdraw $29,412 to generate $25,000 of income.

Third, life insurance policies still provide a death benefit. If the worst-case scenario happens and you die before retirement, your beneficiaries will have a full death benefit to help replace your earnings. If you die in retirement, you'd be able to provide a tax-free benefit to your heirs. If the best-case scenario happens and you may take distributions for 25 years, the policy is still designed to leave something for your heirs.

Investing in a whole life policy for its cash value is an "and" strategy, not an "or" strategy. Implementing this strategy is about maximizing income while taking on less risk and being more tax efficient.

Quick Tip: You may also use an indexed universal life policy for this strategy. There's potential for higher cash value with this strategy, but an indexed universal life policy can be riskier since the cash value it builds is based on a market index such as the S&P 500. Once again, run different illustrations for each type of policy and see which one is a fit for you.

TAKE LOANS DURING A MARKET CORRECTION

A whole life insurance policy's cash value may continue to increase even in a down market. Some life insurance carriers increased their dividend payout rate in 2008 even when the S&P 500 was down over 50%.[26] As I mentioned earlier, taking

---

[26] "Whole Life Dividend Rate History: 1995 to 2020," GBS Life Insurance, accessed July 11, 2022, https://www.gbslife.com/media/29249/dividend-rate-report-2020.pdf.

money from your investments during a down market may compound the harmful effects of a stock market drop. What if you had another income source to withdraw from that wasn't tied to the market?

If the stock market were to drop significantly, you'd be able to take funds out of your whole life policy because the returns of the whole life policy aren't solely based on the returns of the market. Having this pool of funds to withdraw from may give your market-based assets time to recover during a down market. It's like having a relief pitcher come in to pitch when the starter is getting crushed. Let someone else take over for a bit.

How may this work? Let's look at past returns to see. Table 17 shows three outcomes based on three different scenarios:

- Taking distributions each year as you normally would
- Skipping just one distribution the year after the market drop in 2000 (not taking a distribution in 2001)
- Skipping distributions after each year that the market dropped more than 10%, which occurred in 2000, 2001, and 2008 (skipping distributions in 2001, 2002, and 2009)

All three scenarios start with $1,000,000, and each is based on pulling out $40,000 a year plus 2.5% inflation. In the first scenario, you'd have $948,526 left after 22 years; in the second scenario, you'd have over $1.1 million by 2021 (there was an 11.85% drop in the year 2000); and in the third scenario, you'd end up with $1,511,777.

Table 17. *Impact of Skipping Withdrawals after Negative Market Years*

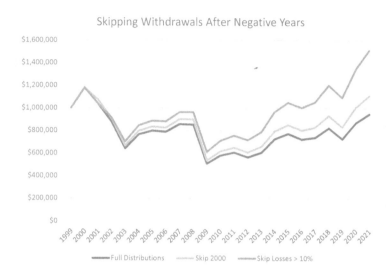

Source: Author, Derek Mazzarella, CFP.

You may be thinking, *Well, if I buy a whole life policy, I won't have as much in my investment account.* Table 18 illustrates how under the same scenario you may have $115,000 less in your retirement account at the start of your retirement, take three distributions from your whole life policy (in 2002, 2003, and 2009), and still end up with roughly the same amount as the investment-only approach. Which retirement would you prefer?

Table 18. *Skipping Withdrawals With a Lower Starting Amount*

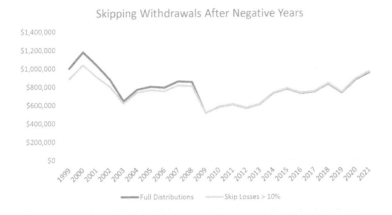

Source: Author, Derek Mazzarella, CFP.

Keep in mind that with an integrated life insurance strategy, you'll still have a death benefit and may take the distributions as loans, which would be tax free. The biggest benefit of an integrated strategy is the psychological benefit. How much would your accounts have to lose before you get concerned? Knowing you have a buffer (non-correlated asset) to withdraw from that isn't impacted by market performance may be incredibly comforting.

If you decide to use this strategy, it's best to create rules for when you'd access the funds from your whole life policy. Use a market drop percentage, such as 10 or 15%+ as a trigger amount, so you build some consistency in the strategy. Utilize the cash in your short-term bucket for year one, and then use your life insurance policy to fill up year two and maintain your cash cushion.

Table 19 shows a hypothetical example of how you could potentially implement this strategy using a 15% drop as your trigger amount.

Table 19. *Hypothetical Withdrawal Example*

Year	Portfolio Return	Income Source
1	12%	Cash Bucket
2	-16%	Cash Bucket
3	10%	Buffer Asset—Life Insurance
4	-5%	Cash Bucket

Don't try to time the use of the buffer asset within the same year as a market drop. Instead, you may use the cash you have in your short-term bucket to fund expenses for the current year, and then use the buffer asset to fund your needed retirement income the year following the market drop.

CHALLENGES AND CAVEATS

While an integrated strategy may be a helpful tool for mitigating retirement risks and improving retirement outcomes, using life insurance in retirement isn't a fit for everyone. Life insurance costs and returns are based on a person's individual health situation and particular time frames. Obtaining life insurance based on your health history is not a guarantee. A poor health history may not exclude you from getting coverage, but it may make the policy too expensive for either of these strategies to be beneficial for you. Implementing this strategy too late in life may not work either. Generally, leveraging a permanent life policy is a long-term strategy and may require funding the policy for at certain number of years. If I may stress one thing, it's that life insurance is based on your individual situation. Run the numbers to ensure this strategy would be a fit for you.

Chapter Highlights

- Integrating non-correlated assets into a retirement income strategy may help increase income and decrease market risk.
- There are three strategies you may use when incorporating permanent life insurance into your retirement plan:
  1. Leverage the death benefit and perhaps incorporate an income-generating annuity.
  2. Overfund the policy and use the cash value as an income source.
  3. Use the policy's cash value during a market correction.
- Whole life insurance policies have returns similar to bonds, but they aren't directly tied to the market.
- Via loans, permanent life insurance policies may provide tax-efficient growth and tax-free withdrawals.
- Investing in permanent life insurance may work better when you have a plan in place for your policy.
- The death benefit from a life insurance policy may provide an extra cushion for a retiree's heirs.
- Integrated strategies may work better when you have the right time horizon and health status.
- Permanent life insurance is not a fit for everyone. Make sure to run the numbers for yourself.

CHAPTER 14

THERE'S ALWAYS MONEY IN THE BANANA STAND

Retirement Tool: Reverse Mortgages
Retirement Risks: Sequence of Returns, Market, Taxes, Longevity

If you've ever stayed home during the day and watched daytime TV, you may have seen a commercial targeted to a retiree, such as Life Alert˚, burial life insurance, or a stair lift. You may have also seen a commercial referencing reverse mortgages and never thought much about them. Before you change the channel next time, you may want to take a few minutes to reexamine how you may utilize a reverse mortgage as a part of your retirement income plan. Much like a permanent life insurance policy, reverse mortgages may act as buffer assets and help you use the equity in your home to create supplemental retirement income outside of the machinations of the stock market.

WHAT IS A REVERSE MORTGAGE?

I'm a fan of the show *Arrested Development*. In season 1, episode 2, the character George Bluth tells his son Michael,

"There is always money in the banana stand."[27] Michael is confused by what his father is telling him, and the banana stand burns down at the end of the episode. It turns out there was backup cash in the banana stand in case they ever needed it. For a retiree, their home is their banana stand (just don't let it burn down). Generally, retirees do have at least some amount of equity in their home.

Traditionally, when a homeowner wants to get cash out of their home, they may either take out a home equity line of credit or use a cash-out refinance. A reverse mortgage is another way to take equity out of your home. Unlike a mortgage, a reverse mortgage means the bank will pay you for the equity in your home. Ultimately, you're only required to pay back up to the value of your home, even if you've borrowed more than your home's value.

How Do You Pay Back a Reverse Mortgage?

There's no free lunch with a reverse mortgage. You'll have to pay the outstanding loan back at some point, normally when you're no longer a full-time resident of your home. You may pay off the loan in one of three ways:

1. Pay off the loan with cash or check.
2. Sell the home and use the proceeds to pay off the loan.
3. Give the lender the ability to sell the home.

Many people will use options two and three to pay off their loan. It's important to note, however, that if you do owe

---

[27]   *Arrested Development*, season 1, episode 2, "Top Banana," directed by Anthony Russo, written by Mitchell Jurwitz, John Levenstein, and Abraham Higginbothem (story editor), featuring Jason Bateman, Portia de Rossi, and Will Arnett, aired November 9, 2003, in broadcast syndication, 20th Century Fox, 2004, DVD.

more than your home is worth, the lender may not go after any of your other assets. The negative loan balance is covered by a mortgage insurance fund from the Federal Housing Administration.

Are You Eligible?

You'd assume that anyone who owns a home would be eligible for a reverse mortgage, but that isn't the case. Here are the eligibility requirements for a reverse mortgage:

- You and any other title holder must be at least 62 years old.
- The reverse mortgage may be your only lien (i.e., you must own the home in full or have a small enough remaining mortgage that it may be paid off).
- You must receive financial counseling.
- Your home needs to be your full-time residence.
- The home must be a single family, two- to four-unit house, and you need to either occupy one of the units or live in a condo approved by the US Department of Housing and Urban Development.

Throughout the reverse mortgage process, you'll also need to keep paying for your property taxes, insurance, and regular home maintenance.

Options Available for Accessing Funds

1. **Lump Sum Payment**: You may take the entire loan value out any time after your reverse mortgage has been approved.
2. **Line of Credit:** You may borrow against a line of credit whenever you need it. This works very similar to a home equity line of credit.

3. **Term**: You collect payments over a specified period of time.

4. **Tenure:** You receive payments over the life of the reverse mortgage or basically as long as you live in your home.

With a variety of payment options available, consider a reverse mortgage if you feel your individual situation permits. I'd suggest speaking with a professional that is versed in this subject before taking any action.

Supplemental Retirement Income

Many people hate having a mortgage, with the fire of a thousand burning suns. Too dramatic? A number of people I interact with are anxiously awaiting the day they no longer have a mortgage payment. Inevitably, they try to pay down their mortgage at a much faster rate. They invest excess income, bonus checks, and tax refunds to pay down their mortgage early. Generally, people don't want to have a mortgage payment in retirement. Paying down the mortgage early comes with a tradeoff, though: fewer liquid assets in retirement. In lieu of putting excess cash into a retirement plan or an investment account, they put the funds toward their house.

When retirement comes around, these people may find themselves in a position of needing more income than their assets will be able to generate on their own. Traditionally, if you were short on income, you may have been forced to sell your home and downsize. Conventional wisdom says we should treat reverse mortgages as a last resort. My thought is: What would happen if you treated the equity in your home as a buffer asset or utilized the reverse mortgage as a supplemental source of income in retirement?

The overall goal of retirement for most people is to create income, not to acquire assets. Once you're at retirement age, you'll need to determine how to maximize your income based on your assets. If most of your assets are tied up in the value of your home, a home equity line may help you create a supplemental income stream. For a hypothetical example, a fully paid off house worth $500,000 may generate over $1,000 a month in income as a tenure payment. For as long as you're able to stay in your home, that income should come in each month no matter what's going on with the stock market. Oh, and income from a reverse mortgage is tax free and usually not considered income, so you'll have that going for you.

Buffer Asset

If you're in the position where you aren't able to get a permanent insurance policy or would rather use the equity in your home, you may set up a line of credit from your reverse mortgage. Use the same set of rules as explained in chapter 13 under the Take Loans During a Market Correction section, and you may withdraw from your line of credit when the market drops a specific percentage (10–15% or more).

Retirement Backstop

You may be in a position where you feel as though you'll have enough money for retirement. Let's say something does go awry, whether that's a prolonged down market, several unexpected expenses, or living longer than expected. A reverse mortgage can give you the ability to tap the equity from your home to supplement your income.

While you may think it would make sense to not take the reverse mortgage out until you need it, doing so could mean losing out on a key feature of reverse mortgages. Unlike most other lines of credit, a reverse mortgage's loan amount will increase over time. Any unused portion of your line of credit will grow by the same adjustable interest rate you'd be charged for a withdrawal. For example, if you take out a line of credit for $150,000, your line of credit amount will grow by the current interest rate. Basically, your line of credit amount will grow over time if you don't borrow from it right away. If you're considering using a reverse mortgage at some point in your retirement, it may be better to initiate your line of credit early on.

With a reverse mortgage, you may plan on initiating the line of credit, letting that credit grow over the course of your retirement, and withdrawing a pool of money from it if and when you need it. Knowing you have access to funds later in life gives you the permission to withdraw from your assets at a potentially greater rate than you'd normally plan on. Either way, before deciding what makes sense, run the numbers based on your situation. There are substantial fees for establishing a reverse mortgage, so be sure you understand the costs.

Tax Planning

As mentioned in chapter 7, people generally find themselves with two different types of tax issues in retirement: they're either on the lower end of the tax spectrum or looking for ways to reduce their taxes. Income received from a reverse mortgage is not taxable and does not count toward your income for Medicare Part B calculations or your combined income calculations for social security. If you find yourself on the lower end of the spectrum, you may use income from a reverse mortgage to keep your social security payments tax free and at the bottom of the Medicare Part B cost bracket.

If you're looking for ways to reduce taxes in retirement, reverse mortgages may be used as a part of your tax-efficient retirement-withdrawal strategy. You would most likely still have to pay taxes on your social security benefits, but you could use supplemental income from a reverse mortgage to help keep the cost of your Medicare Part B premiums down and potentially pay fewer taxes. No matter your tax situation, you may consider a reverse mortgage if you receive social security or Medicare, but more importantly discuss your tax situation with a tax professional before taking any action.

CAVEATS AND CONCERNS

Though reverse mortgages aren't the boogie man that many believe them to be, they certainly come with a few issues to consider:

- Fees and closing costs for reverse mortgages may be high.
  - Origination fees may be as high as $6,000.
  - You'll have mortgage premium insurance costs, which are roughly 2% of your home's value plus a monthly premium of 0.5% of the loan balance.
  - Closing costs compare similarly to traditional mortgages, which include items such as appraisal fees, title searches and/or insurance, and credit checks.
- There are scammers out there, so be aware of them and make sure you're working with a reputable company. You may check for a list of lenders that are approved by the Federal Housing Administration here: https://www.hud.gov/program_offices/housing/sfh/hecm/hecmlenders.
- Make sure you clearly understand the fees, regulations, and expectations of the lender you choose.

- Consider the impact on a non-borrowing spouse. They may outlive the borrowing spouse and not have the funds to pay off the loan.
- If you live with someone whose name isn't on the mortgage, they may not stay in your home if you move out for more than a year or when you die.
- Loan interest may add up over time, and you may be unable to pass your house on to your heirs if the loan interest is greater than your home's value.
- Make sure you keep paying your property taxes and homeowner's insurance. You need to keep your home in good condition, or you could face foreclosure.

Overall, getting a reverse mortgage won't be a fit for everyone, but it's an alternative way for a retiree to access the equity in their home. Carefully consider your options, actually read the reverse mortgage documents before you sign them, and have a plan for how you will use a reverse mortgage before you commit to anything. Remember, there is always money in the banana stand.

Chapter Highlights

- Reverse mortgages may potentially provide a supplemental source of income in retirement.
- To qualify for a reverse mortgage, you must meet the specific criteria.
- There are four ways to access the equity in a reverse mortgage: lump sum payment, line of credit, term, or tenure.
- You may utilize a reverse mortgage as consistent non-market-based income, a buffer asset, a retirement backstop, or money that you receive that is tax-free and not usually considered income.

- When considering a reverse mortgage, be sure you're aware of the high fees, contractual obligations, and risks to your family.28

---

28   If you're considering a reverse mortgage, the Department of Housing and Urban Development (HUD) has two requirements: A meeting with an unbiased, HUD-approved counselor who'll help you make an informed decision by: (1) reviewing the costs and features of different types of reverse mortgages, (2) evaluating the pros and cons of a reverse mortgage for your situation, and (3) understanding the public and private benefits that could help you stay in your home longer. To find a counselor near you, call (800) 569-4287 or visit www. hudexchange.info/programs/housing-counseling/customer-service-feedback. A financial assessment is similar to the underwriting process in a traditional mortgage.

CHAPTER 15

WAIT, SO I GIVE THEM MONEY, THEN THEY GIVE MY MONEY BACK?

Retirement Tool: Annuities
Retirement Risks: Market, Sequence of Returns, Longevity, Taxes

One of the characteristics that made the Terminator a good villain was his relentlessness. No matter what anyone did, the Terminator kept coming. Bullets didn't stop him, cars didn't stop him, and most other outside forces couldn't stop him. In my opinion, annuities are the Terminator of retirement income. They will keep making income payments regardless of whether the stock market is down, what the interest rates are, or who is president.

Back in the day when pensions ruled the world, retirees used to receive consistent monthly income. Pension payments would continue regardless of market performance or how long a person lived. Now that most of us are on our own, we're forced to create our own pensions. One way to do that is by transferring a portion of your assets to annuities.

When used correctly, annuities may help reduce market risk, sequence of returns risk, and longevity risk, and they may be tax efficient. Unlike life insurance, annuities don't require you to be healthy to buy them (although with some annuities it's better if you're healthy). With annuities there's always a tradeoff: you may give up some return or liquidity or pay higher fees, but adding annuities to your retirement income plan may help build in more security and certainty. Annuities may help raise your floor.

At a high level, annuities can have two different jobs: providing a return while reducing or eliminating market risk, and providing lifetime income. Choosing which annuity is right for you, if any, may be confusing, but starting with what goal you'd like to accomplish may help narrow your options. There are four main types of annuities, and each has its own unique pros and cons. Like any other financial tool, each annuity has its place. Here's a breakdown of the four different annuities, what they are best used for, and their downsides.

SINGLE PREMIUM IMMEDIATE ANNUITY (SPIA)

I touched on SPIAs in chapter 13, but I want to dig a little deeper here. SPIAs are the most straightforward annuity option. With an SPIA, you give the insurance carrier money, and they'll immediately give you income for the rest of your life—no matter how long you live. The catch here is that when you die, the carrier keeps your money, but SPIAs generally offer the highest payouts compared to other annuity options (see figure 10).

SPIA Payments Over Time

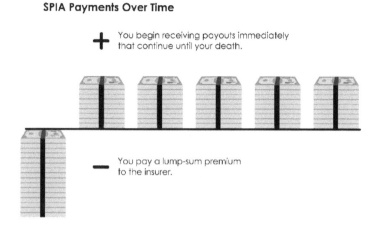

Figure 10: Illustrated SPIA Example

If the thought of giving your money to an insurance carrier with nothing going to your beneficiaries scares you, you may utilize several SPIA payout options.

- **Life Only:** Payments are made as long as you live. Once you die, there's no death benefit.
- **Joint Life:** Payments are made until the last spouse dies.
- **Life Period Certain:** Payments are made for the annuitant's life, but if they die before the period is up, payments will continue. For example, if someone chooses "10-year period certain" and the annuitant dies after six years of payments, the beneficiary will receive payments for four more years.

The highest payout will come from the life-only option. The more certainty you add to the payments after the annuitant dies, the lower your payment will be, meaning that if the insurance carrier must pay someone else after you die, your payments will be lower.

Downsides

There are four main downsides to be aware of with SPIAs. First, while they do offer a higher payment, most aren't linked to inflation. This means the payment will stay flat throughout the rest of your life. If the SPIA does offer a link to inflation, then your initial payment will be lower. Second, your initial payment will be based on interest rates at the time you purchase the SPIA. Buying an SPIA in a low-interest-rate environment means you could potentially lock in a low payment. Third, the breakeven point for SPIAs is generally between 15 and 17 years. Depending on the payout option you choose, if you choose a life-only payment, you might die before the breakeven point, causing your beneficiaries to receive nothing. Fourth, most other annuities offer similar lifetime income payouts and provide the ability to leave any remaining account balance to a beneficiary.

When to Use Them

My grandfather lived to 100, and my great-grandmother lived to 106. They both would have blown past the breakeven point and cost the insurance carrier some money because they would have made twice what they invested in their SPIA.

If you're healthy and have longevity in your family, an SPIA may be a good option for you. Getting a lifetime payment will help you mitigate longevity risk since it's impossible to run out of money. SPIAs may also help reduce market risk and sequence of returns risk because payments from an SPIA aren't tied to the market; whether the market is up or down, you'd continue to receive the same payment. For some people, having monthly income is better than having a lump sum of money so that they can't spend it too quickly. You know who you are.

FIXED ANNUITY

Fixed annuities are the training-wheels version of annuities. They offer a "safe" return with no market risk. A fixed annuity offers a fixed interest rate each year for a set number of years (generally three to seven). They will usually offer a slightly better return than a CD and are highly dependent on interest rates. If interest rates are low, the returns will be low; if interest rates are high, the returns will be higher.

Downsides

If you decide to invest in a fixed annuity, you'll get a risk-free rate of return but will lose some access or liquidity. Generally, fixed annuities offer a low rate of return compared to most other investment options. Many fixed annuities have a minimum surrender period (time when you may access your money) of at least three years.

When to Use Them

Fixed annuities are generally a fit for very conservative investors who don't want to lose their money. I don't often recommend these in a low-interest-rate environment, but if you don't need liquidity, they're a better investment option compared to cash. If you're a person who's too scared of the market and likes to keep your money in cash, they might be a fit for you.[29]

---

[29]   Fixed annuities are long-term investment vehicles designed for retirement purposes. Gains from tax-deferred investments are taxable as ordinary income upon withdrawal. Guarantees are based on the claims paying ability of the issuing company. Withdrawals made prior to age 59 ½ are subject to a 10% IRS penalty tax and surrender charges may apply.

INDEXED ANNUITIES & RILAS

When little kids are just learning to swim, they can't quite go into the water on their own yet. When they do go in the water, we put floaties on them. They may not be able to swim as fast with the floaties on, but they are protected from drowning. Indexed annuities are the floaties of the financial world. They give you the ability to participate in some of the upsides of the stock market and either eliminate or reduce exposure to negative returns.

Indexed annuities are a more complicated investment than most. They may be challenging to understand, and each indexed annuity is slightly different depending on the annuity carrier. At a high level, indexed annuities will put floors and ceilings on stock market returns. At a more detailed level, they involve some specific terms.

- **Participation Rate:** A participation rate is the percentage of the stock market index growth that an indexed annuity credits to your annuity's subaccount. For example, if the S&P 500 returned 10% and the participation rate was 70%, an indexed annuity would show you earned 7%. One catch with indexed annuities is they don't include dividends in their calculation. Historically, dividends have returned between 1.5 and 2% annually. Indexed annuities only base returns off of the price return.
- **Rate Cap:** A rate cap is the maximum amount that an annuity carrier will credit your subaccount. If the cap is 10% and the S&P 500 returned 25%, your index annuity will have grown by 10%. If the index's return is under the cap, you'll receive that return.
- **Buffer:** A buffer is how much of a stock market loss the annuity carrier will cover for you. If the buffer is

10% and the market is down 15%, you'd lose 5%. If the market was down 5%, you'd lose nothing. Buffers cover either the first 5, 10, 15, or 20% of losses depending on the option you choose.

- **Floor:** A floor represents the most you'd lose with your indexed annuity. In most cases the floor is 0%, meaning you wouldn't lose anything if the market had a loss even if the loss was 30% or more.

- **Point to Point:** Point to point is an evaluation of the value of your annuity from a start date and an end date. The point to point usually aligns with when you sign the annuity contract. For example, if your annuity contract date is April 25th, then your next evaluation point would be April 25th of the following year. Point to points may be monthly, quarterly, or annually.

Figure 11 illustrates how indexed annuities may work. Even though market returns may be higher or lower than the cap and floor, respectively, your returns with an indexed annuity will be within the floor and cap.

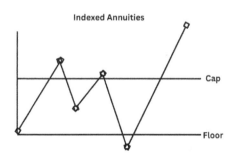

Indexed Annuities

Figure 11: Illustrated Fixed Indexed Annuity Example

Registered indexed linked annuities (RILAs) have come along more recently and offer a different take on providing some market exposure while trying to limit the impacts of a down stock market. Like indexed annuities, RILAs may have caps, floors, and/or buffers, but they also have the option of crediting your annuity over a six-year period versus a one-year point-to-point situation. Compared to an indexed annuity, RILAs may be a fit for those looking for more market upside since they tend to offer higher caps.

Downsides

As I mentioned earlier, there are a few negatives to indexed annuities, and they may be complicated to understand. They limit your upside with caps on gains, which means your long-term returns will usually underperform stocks. Dividend payments aren't included in the return and, like other annuities, aren't fully liquid right away. There's a penalty for withdrawing money before the surrender date, although some will have a 10% penalty-free withdrawal. Fixed annuities may also include higher fees and commissions.

When to Use Them

Indexed annuities and RILAs may be a good fit for when you're trying to obtain some stock market growth but don't want to take on the full risk of the stock market. You may also utilize them as bond alternatives, just keep in mind that they tend to work better in that capacity in a low-interest-rate environment.

VARIABLE ANNUITY

Historically, variable annuities may give you the most investment freedom of any of the previously mentioned annuity products. You can invest in an array of mutual funds called subaccounts, which may be as aggressive or conservative as you like. You may have the ability to annuitize the variable annuity. Annuitizing a variable annuity provides lifetime income in the same vein as an SPIA.

For an additional fee, some variable annuities offer "riders," or additional features that may be added to the annuity, like heated seats in a car. One of the most common riders we see is called a "guaranteed lifetime withdrawal benefit," or GLWB. GLWBs may be complicated to understand, but they give you the ability to invest in the stock market and have a source of lifetime income that will grow over time, even if the market doesn't do well. The GLWB rider works like a ratchet, locking in gains each policy anniversary.

When someone invests in a variable annuity, the carrier keeps tabs on two accounts: the account value and the GLWB value. The account value is your "walking away" money, or the amount you may take from the annuity, much like you would with an investment account. The GLWB value, however, may be taken *only* as income over time. Think of an investment property. You may either collect the equity when you sell the property (account value) or collect the rent (GLWB), but you can't do both at the same time.

For example, let's say a person invests $100,000 into a variable annuity with a GLWB rider that has a growth rate of 5%. The carrier will lock in either the market return or the GLWB growth rate, whichever is higher. Table 20 shows how that would look if the market outperformed the 5% growth rate.

Table 20. *Hypothetical GLWB Return Example*

Year	Starting Balance	Investment Return	Account Value	GLWB Value
1	$100,000	10%	$110,000	$110,000
2	$110,000	6%	$116,600	$116,600
3	$116,600	12%	$130,592	$130,592

*This is a hypothetical example and is not representative of any specific situation. Your results will vary. The hypothetical rates of return used do not reflect the deduction of fees and charges.

In this example, the GLWB rider is locking in the same value as the account value because the market is outperforming the 5% growth rate. What would happen if there were a down year? See Table 21.

Table 21. *Hypothetical GLWB Return Example with a Negative Return*

Year	Starting Balance	Investment Return	Account Value	GLWB Value
1	$100,000	10%	$110,000	$110,000
2	$110,000	-6%	$103,400	$115,500
3	$103,400	12%	$115,808	$121,275

*This is a hypothetical example and is not representative of any specific situation. Your results will vary. The hypothetical rates of return used do not reflect the deduction of fees and charges.

Because the market return was higher than the 5% credit rate, the GLWB rider locks in the 10% market gain in year one. With a negative 6% return in year two, the impact of the 5% growth rate of the GLWB rider is clear: while the account value drops due to negative market performance, the GLWB value increases. We may even see the impact of not losing in year three: the GLWB value with a 5% return is higher compared to the market return of 12%. The GLWB rider ensures your ability to take income from the GLWB value never decreases because of a negative market performance. To be clear, the GLWB value is used only to calculate lifetime income. The annuity carrier would take 5 or 6% of the GLWB value, for example, and that would be your income for life.

Downsides

There are a few issues to keep in mind when it comes to variable annuities. First, there are more fees associated with variable annuities compared to other investments. With variable annuities, there are mortality and expense fees (1 to 1.5%), investment/mutual fund fees (0.5 to 1%), and a fee for the GLWB rider itself (~1%). All in all, you may expect to pay about 2.5 to 3.5% with a variable annuity, depending on what riders you add to the annuity and what you invest in.

Second, variable annuities may be complicated to understand. There are numerous riders to explore, fees to uncover, and rules with certain carriers to understand. For example, some annuity carriers restrict how aggressive you may be with your investments. They may cap your allocation to 60 or 70% in stocks, which could reduce your returns. Some carriers also charge fees based on your highest account value, which accelerates how quickly your account value may drop to zero. It won't matter if you're taking income from the account, but it will reduce how much you may pass on to your beneficiaries.

Third, any growth in a non-qualified variable annuity will be taxed at income tax rates rather than capital gains rates. If your income is lower or close to the capital gains rate, this may not be an issue, but this could be costly if your effective tax rate is higher when you take withdrawals.

When to Use Them

Variable annuities may be useful in two instances. First, if you're looking for a source of tax deferral, a variable annuity can provide you with market participation, but you won't be subject to annual tax bills as with an investment account. Depending on the size of your investment account and your time horizon, a variable annuity could save you thousands in taxes over the years. Second, a variable annuity with a GLWB rider allows you to tackle sequence of returns risk, market risk, and longevity risk all at once. If you're a few years away from needing to take income, this method may provide market participation and insurance in case there's a down market around your retirement date. Generally, the most dangerous time for a market downturn for a retiree is the five years before and after they retire.

The GLWB rider may provide retirement income for the rest of your life and give you a higher payout compared to the "traditional withdrawal rate" of 4%, even if your account value goes to zero. It may also be an alternative to an SPIA. Unlike an SPIA, a variable annuity allows you to pass on any remaining account value balance to your beneficiaries.[30]

---

30 Variable Annuities are suitable for long-term investing, such as retirement investing. Withdrawals prior to age 59 ½ may be subject to tax penalties and surrender charges may apply. Variable annuities are subject to market risk and may lose value. Riders are additional guarantee options that are available to an annuity or life insurance contract holder. While some riders are part of an existing contract, many others may carry additional fees, charges and restrictions, and the policy holder should review their contract carefully before purchasing. Guarantees are based on the claims paying ability of the issuing insurance company.

Using Annuities As Part of Your Retirement Income Portfolio Strategy

Remember, increasing the potential enjoyment of your retirement is all about raising your floor. Annuities may provide an opportunity to maintain similar stock and bond portfolio returns while passing some of the risk to an insurance carrier. They may also provide an avenue of consistent income for your retirement. Here are two examples of how you may integrate annuities into your retirement plan based on your objective.

Your Goal is Safety of Returns

Conventional wisdom will tell you that you need to "de-risk" your portfolio as you get closer and into retirement. Retirees traditionally use bonds to potentially reduce market risk. While bonds do provide some safety with their coupon payment, they may still lose value. Though bonds certainly have their place, what would happen if you were to replace a *portion* of your bond portfolio with an indexed annuity? Remember, retirement planning is all about "and" not "or."

To answer this question, economist Roger Ibbotson ran a study evaluating the historical returns of stocks, bonds, and indexed annuities. He found that indexed annuities have a historical return similar to bonds but with less risk because most indexed annuities have a floor of 0%. After evaluating the results of altering a 60/40 portfolio with a portfolio that was 60/20/20 (60% stocks, 20% bonds, and 20% indexed annuity), Ibbotson discovered that the returns were better with the latter.[31] Those findings make sense since ~74% of the time

---

[31]   Roger G. Ibbotson, "Fixed Indexed Annuities: Consider the Alternatives," Zebra Capital Management & Yale School of Finance, January 2018, https://

stocks have a positive return, and over time stocks will outperform bonds.[32] In a low-interest-rate environment, bonds may also have negative returns and periods of low returns. Indexed annuities and RILAs have historically outperformed bonds when the market is up and outperformed stocks when the stock market is down, thus providing a balance to the volatility of the market.

One criticism people have of Ibbotson's study is that he used a hypothetical indexed annuity. Considering that annuity products are constantly changing, back-testing strategies is a challenging endeavor. We may still learn a lot from past markets, however. While past markets are never exactly the same, they do rhyme with current ones.

Ultimately, you'll have to decide whether this type of strategy is right for you. Make sure you understand all the positive and negative aspects of index/RILA annuities. Consider the type of market you're in, what the current interest-rate environment is, and when you'd need to access the funds. As always, run the numbers for yourself or with the help of a financial advisor to make sure this strategy would be a fit for you. As always, work with your tax professional regarding your individual situation.

---

www.zebracapital.com/wp-content/uploads/2019/06/Fixed-Indexed-Annuities-Consider-the-Alternative-January-2018.pdf.

[32] NYU School of Business, "Historical Returns on Stocks, Bonds, and Bills: 1928–2022." NYU School of Business. May 30, 2023, https://pages.stern.nyu.edu/~adamodar/New_Home_Page/datafile/histretSP.html.

You Need Stable Income

Compared to traditional stock and bond investments, annuities come with three main benefits:

1. Annuities may pay a higher payout rate compared to the "safe withdrawal rate."
2. Annuity income payments are not subject to market risk.
3. Annuities may offer payments for the rest of your life.

Unlike CDs, bonds, stocks, or other traditional investments, most annuities will pay you income based on your age; the older you are, the more the annuity carrier will pay you (see table 22). You can't call up Verizon and ask for a higher dividend payout because you turned 70.

Table 22. *SPIA Annuity Payout Rate by Age*

Age	Annuity Payout Rate (SPIA)
65	7.74%
70	8.67%
75	9.94%

Note: Results based on AIG SPIA rates calculated on January 5th, 2023, for a male.

Annuity carriers may do this because of mortality credits. From an individual standpoint, we'll all die at different ages; some of us will live to age 96, and some will live to age 70. Collectively, the insurance carrier knows that if it may get enough people to pool their money, it will be able to predict the life expectancy of the entire pool. The carrier may end up paying more for one person and less for another. The people who die at 70 essentially pay for the people who live to age 96.

Lifetime income from an annuity may help you mitigate market risk and sequence of returns risk because you'll continue getting payments from the annuity carrier no matter how the market is doing. It also helps mitigate longevity risk because you won't be able to outlive your money. For example, if you give the annuity carrier $100,000, they pay you $7,500 a year, and you live for 25 more years, you'll collect $187,500 because they're contractually obligated to keep paying you.

There are several annuity options to choose from, and picking one that makes sense for you may potentially add greater certainty to your retirement. Just like in the movies, it may be helpful to have the Terminator on your side.

Quick Tip: Many of the previously mentioned annuities offer riders that will generate lifetime income, which accomplishes the same goal as an SPIA. The payments may not be as high as with an SPIA, but the annuities will generally give any remaining account value to your beneficiaries. Be sure to evaluate a few different annuity options to see which one, if any, is right for you.

Chapter Highlights

- Annuities may help fill the void left by the death of pensions.
- There are four main types of annuities:
  1. Single premium immediate annuities (SPIAs), which are used to generate income
  2. Fixed annuities, which are used when you need a guaranteed return
  3. Indexed annuities and RILAs, which are used to get some stock market upside and provide some downside protection
  4. Variable annuities, which are used when you want investment flexibility and/or tax deferral and may be a source of income with the GLWB income rider

- You may use annuities to provide safety of returns by integrating them into your overall portfolio.
- To ensure you have payments for life, you may leverage annuities to generate a higher payout rate while working to remove market risk and sequence of returns risk.

CHAPTER 16

LOCATION, LOCATION, LOCATION

Retirement Tool: Asset Location
Retirement Risk: Taxes

Think about the food you have in your house. Some foods make sense to keep in the fridge, and some you keep in the pantry. If you went to your friend's house and noticed they kept crackers in the freezer and milk in the pantry, you may start rethinking your friendship. The same thing may be true when it comes to where you store your investments, except instead of them simply spoiling or it generally being weird, your tax bill could be impacted.

The type of account you decide to keep your investments in may have an impact on the amount of taxes you pay now and in retirement. Since taxes make up a significant expense in both instances, you should try to do everything you may to minimize that expense.

The first step in crafting an effective tax strategy is understanding how money is taxed. Most money is held in three types of accounts, each of which has a separate tax treatment:

1. **Qualified Accounts** (e.g., traditional IRAs, 401(k)s, 403(b)s, etc.), which are funded with money that is tax deductible, have an account value that may grow over time and be tax deferred, and require distributions to be taxed.
2. **Roth Accounts** (e.g., Roth IRAs, Roth 401(k)s, 457s, permanent life insurance [if loans are used]), which are funded with after-tax dollars, have an account value that grows tax free, and don't require distributions to be taxed.
3. **Non-Qualified Accounts** (e.g., investment accounts, real estate, businesses), which are funded with after-tax dollars, are taxed annually, and require tax on distributions if there's growth (at either capital gains rates or income tax rates).

Figure 12 presents a visual of these three account types.

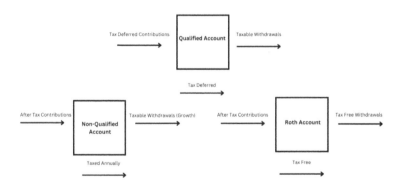

Figure 12: How Money Is Taxed in Three Types of Accounts

Now that you know how taxes work at the account type level, the next question becomes, "What are the best assets to put into each account?" Some assets are more tax efficient than others. For example, income from a corporate bond will be taxed at income tax rates, and qualified dividend payments from stocks are taxed at 0, 15, or 20%, depending on your tax bracket. Let's look at two funds as an example (see table 23). One is a growth fund made up of stocks, and the other is a bond fund. If your tax rate is 24%, which asset makes the most sense to hold in a Roth compared to an investment account?

Table 23. *Tax Location Comparison*

Fund	Roth IRA Tax Rate	Investment Account Tax Rate
Stock	0%	15%
Bond	0%	24%

Since the Roth IRA offers tax-free growth, you would want to hold the fund with the higher tax liability in the Roth IRA, which in this case is the bond fund. The stock fund would be better held in the investment account. There's a 9% difference in the taxation of the two assets based on which account holds the asset.

Asset location may seem like a small thing, but financial planning is all about finding small advantages over time. The larger the account size, the more these tax moves matter. The key to minimizing taxes now and in retirement is putting the right type of asset in the most beneficial account type. In other words, put the milk in the fridge and the crackers in the pantry. Everyone's situation will be different. If you're in a low tax bracket, it may make sense to hold your growth fund in your Roth IRA and your bond fund in your investment account. See table 24 for a guideline on the most appropriate locations for certain assets.[33]

---

[33] This table is intended as a guideline only; it's best to speak with a tax professional.

Table 24. *Asset Location Guidelines based on Taxes*

Security Type	Tax Treatment of Returns	Non-Qualified (Taxable)	Qualified (Tax Deferred)	Roth (Tax Exempt)
Muni Bonds / Mutual Funds	Generally exempt	***	*	*
Equity Securities Held Long Term	Taxed at long-term capital gains rates	***	**	**
Equity Index Funds / ETFs (Excluding REITs)		***	**	**
Tax-Managed Mutual Funds		***	*	*
Real Estate Investment Trusts (REITs)	Generally, 80% of income taxed at ordinary income rates and 20% tax exempt	**	***	*
High Turnover Mutual Funds (Short-Term Gain Heavy)	Taxed at ordinary income tax rates	*	***	***
Fully Taxable Bonds and Bond Funds		*	***	***
***More appropriate; **Appropriate; *Less appropriate				

Source: Fidelity Viewpoints, "Are You Invested in the Right Kind of Accounts?" Fidelity, March 9, 2022, https://www.fidelity.com/viewpoints/investing-ideas/asset-location-lower-taxes.

When it comes to asset location planning strategies, there are four items to consider:

1. What is your current marginal income tax rate? Generally, higher marginal income tax rates will see more impact with asset location planning compared to lower income tax rates.
2. What is your expected marginal tax rate in retirement? Projecting your future expected marginal income tax rate may give you an idea of any shifts that may be made now to help minimize taxes now and in the future.
3. What is your investment time frame? The longer your investment time frame, the greater impact asset location planning may have.
4. Where are your assets currently held? Are there any changes you should make to the assets in your respective accounts? Does it make sense to move a tax inefficient asset, such as a REIT, to an IRA?

You may use table 24 to determine whether you need to make any changes to the location of your assets. Be aware, however, that moving assets from one account to another type of account could be considered a sale and may trigger an unwanted taxable event. Overall, if done correctly and with purpose, asset location planning may help reduce your tax liability over time.

Quick Tip: Mutual funds held in non-qualified accounts have a tax quirk that may be important to know: you're responsible for the tax liability incurred by the mutual fund for the entire year, even if you've owned the mutual fund for only a couple of months. Exchange traded funds don't have this issue and from a tax perspective are generally better suited for non-qualified accounts compared to qualified or Roth accounts.

Chapter Highlights

- Taxes may erode wealth over time.
- Most accounts are taxed in one of three ways: qualified, Roth, and non-qualified.
- Tax treatment may be different depending on the type of asset.
- Placing the assets in a more tax-appropriate account may help reduce tax liabilities.
- There are four main items to consider when using asset location planning: current marginal tax rate, future marginal tax rate, investment time frame, and evaluation of the type of account your investments are in.

CHAPTER 17

HOW DO WE GET RID OF THIS?

Retirement Tool: Withdrawal Sequence
Retirement Risk: Taxes

To me, gin on its own tastes terrible. Does anyone take shots of gin? Is that a thing? Maybe I'm drinking the wrong gin. Gin works best when it's blended with other ingredients to make a cocktail. Mix gin, simple syrup, lemon, and club soda, and you have a refreshing Tom Collins. The key to a good cocktail is blending the right ingredients at the proper ratio. Making withdrawals from your accounts in retirement should be treated the same as making a cocktail. Withdrawing the proper amount of money from the right account may make a significant difference on the taxes you'll pay over the course of your retirement.

As I mentioned in chapter 7, retirees don't often have a good strategy for minimizing taxes in retirement. Traditionally we're taught that taxes are a look-back exercise. We frequently try to limit our tax bills from the prior year, but we rarely, if ever, project our taxes into the future. In working years, we're taught to invest in tax "savings" vehicles such as traditional 401(k)s, 403(b)s, or traditional IRAs (qualified accounts), which reduce our income today. When we get to retirement, we're then taught to delay taking from these accounts because they're more tax efficient compared to non-qualified accounts. We're told to postpone our tax bill as long as possible until the government tells us we need to make withdrawals. While that may be effective in the short term, constantly delaying taxes usually means a much larger tax bill later. Our tax bills may be mostly soda water now and too much gin later.

Let's look at a hypothetical example of how delaying taxes until you're required to take them affects a retiree (figure 13). The scenarios are based on a 60-year-old retiring at age 65.

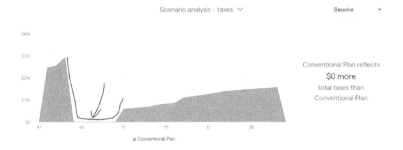

Figure 13: Conventional Withdrawal Sequence. Image generated using RightCapital Financial Planning Software and is based on a 60-year-old retiring at age 65 with $100,000 in a non-qualified account and $650,000 in a qualified account with a retirement lasting until age 90.

Most people will have a "U" shaped retirement when it comes to taxes. Right before retirement, most people are usually in a higher tax bracket. They see a dip in their tax rate in the beginning of their retirement because they're taking money mostly from their investment accounts. A retiree sees their taxes increase due to income from their social security payments and withdrawals from their qualified accounts. Medicare premium payments may increase as well. Sometimes retirees are required to take out more money than they even

119

need. Are there more tax-efficient withdrawal strategies? Let's look at two other options.

PRO RATA WITHDRAWAL

What would happen if a retiree were to create a mixed tax cocktail by blending in withdrawals from different types of tax accounts (qualified and non-qualified)? Instead of waiting until the last possible moment, they take some qualified withdrawals earlier in retirement, leverage the low-income-tax environment of the first few years, and pay a lower tax rate on the qualified funds they take out of their accounts. Figure 14 provides an example outcome using this same hypothetical retiree but with a more tax-efficient withdrawal strategy.

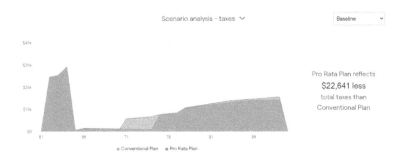

Figure 14: Pro Rata Withdrawal Sequence. Image generated using RightCapital Financial Planning Software and is based on a 60-year-old retiring at age 65 with $100,000 in a non-qualified account and $650,000 in a qualified account and a retirement lasting until age 90. By comparison, the only change is taking an annual distribution of $14,100 from the hypothetical person's 401(k) plan from age 65–74.

In this example, I've changed nothing other than taking $14,100 each year from age 65 through age 74 from the retiree's 401(k) plan. This retiree still took out the same overall amount of money, but they're now taking it from both their investment account and their 401(k). As a result, the retiree's taxes are a little under $22,000 less over the course of their retirement.

ROTH CONVERSION WITHDRAWAL

A second strategy is to consider layering in Roth conversions before RMDs start during early low tax years (see figure 15). Basically, a retiree may fill in a portion of the bottom of their "U" shape by making Roth conversions. Any amount converted from a qualified account to a Roth IRA would be considered income in the year of the conversion.

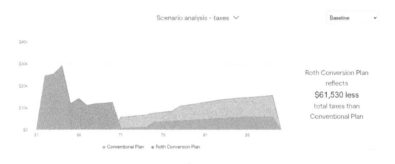

Figure 15: Roth Conversion Withdrawal Sequence. Image generated using RightCapital Financial Planning Software and is based on a 60-year-old retiring at age 65 with $100,000 in a non-qualified account and $650,000 in a qualified account and a retirement lasting until age 90. By comparison, there are two changes: making Roth conversions and pushing collecting social security payments until age 70.

This scenario shows the impacts of converting some of a retiree's 401(k) assets to a Roth IRA. I did make one other change, which was to push back social security payments from age 65 to age 70. Typically, the Roth conversion strategy works best when you delay social security. As a result of the Roth conversions, this retiree's taxes were reduced by almost $61,530 over the course of their retirement.

While your situation will be different from this hypothetical retiree's, the idea here is to show how having a tax
withdrawal strategy may help you reduce your tax liability in
retirement. Figuring out which type of account to withdraw
from *does* matter and *will* impact your retirement. If you're further away from retirement than this hypothetical person, you
have more opportunity for tax planning. In general, the more
time you have until retirement and the lower your income is,
the more you may want to invest in Roth accounts. As you
move forward in your career, you'll most likely be in a higher
tax bracket, and you'll have less time to plan. Figure 16 is a
visual of this concept that you may use as a guideline.

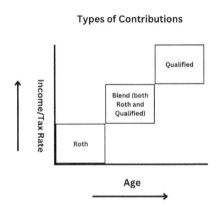

Figure 16: Types of Contributions Over Time

Whichever of these two strategies you go with, saving into
a mix of accounts (Roth, qualified, and non-qualified) gives
you the ability to be more flexible with your withdrawals in
retirement. My examples explore retirement expenses with linear growth, but we all know that expenses may vary from year
to year. One year you may need to redo your roof, or maybe
you'll decide to take a bigger vacation. Having a variety of

accounts to pull from may help you be nimble with your withdrawals and potentially reduce your overall tax liability.

Discovering your best withdrawal strategy will ultimately be up to you. Determining your mix of qualified, Roth, and non-qualified withdrawals will be based on your income sources, timeline, income needs, and any future changes to RMD withdrawal schedules. The main point here is that when it comes to tax planning for retirement, look past one year time segments. Project how much income you'll need in retirement, and measure that against your expected tax brackets. Make a tax cocktail that works best for you.

Chapter Highlights

- Taxes are one of the largest expenses in retirement.
- Retirees are generally taught to delay withdrawing from their qualified (pre-tax) accounts as long as possible.
- Evaluating different withdrawal strategies may help you reduce your overall tax liability over the course of your retirement.
- Taking distributions from a blend of account types on a pro rata basis may help you reduce your tax bill in retirement.
- If you have enough non-qualified assets to cover your income for a few years, you may want to consider converting your IRA funds to Roth IRAs during your low tax years earlier on in retirement.
- Investing in a combination of different types of accounts prior to retirement gives you withdrawal flexibility in retirement.
- Determining the right mix of accounts to save into and withdraw from will be based on your time frame, income level, and expenses.

CHAPTER 18

ANYONE ELSE GOING THROUGH WITHDRAWALS?

Retirement Tool: Dynamic Withdrawals
Retirement Risks: Longevity, Market

I n any marathon or long-distance race, runners must find the right tempo. Too fast and they burn out; too slow and they leave too much on the table. Running a long-distance race at the correct speed takes time, practice, and knowledge of the course. Figuring out how much of your nest egg to spend in retirement is very similar, except you don't know how long your race will be. Not knowing how long your retirement will be is challenging, but you may still find the right pace.

Conventional wisdom says that we should be able to safely withdraw 4% of our retirement assets over the course of a 30-year retirement. If we had one million dollars saved at retirement, we'd be able to generate an income of $40,000 a year. We'd also adjust our income/withdrawals by the inflation rate each year. The 4% rule was created by William (Bill) Bengen in 1994.[34] Since then, he's noted that the withdrawal rate should actually be closer to 4.5%.

---

[34]   William P. Bengen, "Determining Withdrawal Rates Using Historical Data,"

Some critics of the 4% rule mention that bond returns were much higher when Bengen conducted his study. In 2021, for example, Morningstar argued that the "safe" withdrawal rate should be 3.3% with a 50/50 portfolio mix and a 30-year time horizon, but they also note that the withdrawal rate may increase to 4.5% under certain circumstances.[35] So what's a retiree to do?

Financial planners often make assumptions using linear retirement expense numbers, but we all know that life isn't linear. We don't have the same expenses each year, and our expenses change as we age. Some studies mention that retirement spending decreases as we age, while others say retirement spending looks more like a smile: higher expenses early in retirement, lower as you age, then higher again toward the end due to medical costs. Some retirees may even be hesitant to spend down their assets because of behavioral hang ups. They may want to pass money to their children, or they may just like having a "Scrooge McDuck" pile of money. Either way, your retirement spending habits will be unique to you. Let's evaluate some of the variables to consider and break down how you should look at retirement spending.

Journal of Financial Planning, October 1994, 171–180, https://www.retailinvestor.org/pdf/Bengen1.pdf.

[35] Christine Benz, Jefferey Ptak, and John Rekenthaler, "The State of Retirement Income: 2022," Morningstar, December 12, 2022, https://assets.contentstack.io/v3/assets/blt4eb669caa7dc65b2/blt0cdaf6ab25075b47/6398c339313cec5f8f3b5c8a/The_State_Of_Retirement_Income_2022.pdf.

Retirement Withdrawal Variables

Market Returns

It may not come as a surprise to you at this point, but stock markets go through periods of higher and lower returns. The type of market you retire into does matter and could potentially have an impact on your withdrawal rates in retirement. Morningstar looked back at the lowest and highest safe withdrawal rates over different time increments, and figure 17 illustrates how different withdrawal rates may be based on historical markets.[36]

Figure 17: Highest and Lowest Safe Starting Withdrawal Rates by Time Period and Asset Allocation. Results based on a 30-year time horizon and five asset allocations ranging from 100% bonds to 100% stock and with a 90% potential success rate.

---

36   Christine Benz, Jeffrey Ptak, and John Rekenthaler, "The State of Retirement Income: Safe Withdrawal Rates," Morningstar, November 11, 2021, https://www.morningstar.com/content/dam/marketing/shared/pdfs/Research/state-of-retirement-income.pdf.

As you may see from the data, the lowest safe withdrawal rate was 2.4% from 1940 to 1969, and the highest safe withdrawal rate was 6.5% from 1975 to 2004. That difference may represent tens of thousands of dollars each year in retirement income.

How do you know what market you're retiring into? You'll never be 100% accurate, but many money managers, such as Vanguard and J. P. Morgan, will put out capital market assumptions each year. These assumptions try to project future returns based on current market conditions and valuations. They aren't the holy grail of investment projections, and they may be wrong, but they may provide at least a guideline of future returns.

Non-Portfolio Income

Retirees may commonly have up to three different sources of non-portfolio income: social security, pension income, and income from an annuity. And now you know you may throw income from a permanent life policy and potentially depending on your individual situation, a reverse mortgage into this category as well.

Deciding when to take social security will be one of the most pivotal choices you make in retirement. If you decide to delay taking social security, you could put more pressure on your assets earlier on in retirement. If you decide to take social security early, you may need to use a smaller amount of your assets to cover your expenses, but over a longer time frame. Many pensions and annuities won't increase your payments as inflation rises.

No matter what type of non-portfolio income you have, the more income you receive from these sources, the less you'll potentially need to withdraw from your portfolio.

Inflation

Much like the stock market, inflation fluctuates over time and during different economic cycles. Obviously, low inflation is better for a retiree than high inflation. The higher the inflation rate, the less buying power your assets will have in retirement. Those who retired in the early 2000s through 2010 were able to experience a prolonged period of low inflation that put less pressure on their assets. In contrast, inflation averaged 7.08% in the 1970s, which added an additional challenge for anyone retiring at that time.[37]

Inflation may have a subtle impact on retirement. For example, let's compare an inflation rate of 3% to an inflation rate of 5% over a 20-year period and see how they would apply to groceries. If you spent $100 a week on groceries, you'd spend $5,200 a year. How would the cost of those groceries increase with different inflation rates? See table 25.

Table 25. *Impacts of Inflation Over Time*

	3% Inflation	5% Inflation
Current	$5,200	$5,200
10 Years	$6,785	$7,683
20 Years	$9,118	$13,140

If you apply inflation to other costs in your life, you may see how higher inflation rates may put more pressure on your retirement portfolio's ability to generate income.

"Historical Inflation Rates: 1914–2022," U.S. Inflation Calculator, accessed July 18, 2022, https://www.usinflationcalculator.com/inflation/historical-inflation-rates/.

Time Horizon

Time horizons are the impossible question. How long is each of us going to live? If we knew that answer, planning for retirement would be easy. A safe withdrawal looks at retirement time horizons of 30 years. The reality is that many people won't have a retirement that lasts 30 years, but what if *yours* does? The unknown is why we tend to be conservative with these numbers; as financial advisors, we don't want you to run out of money.

If you'd like to be a little more precise, you may try to evaluate your own mortality by looking at your family history of health, longevity, weight, and lifestyle choices (e.g., drugs, alcohol, smoking, diet, exercise). If you feel as though you may not live past the average life expectancy, it's worth exploring the option of taking more money out than a person who's expected to live longer. If you have longevity on your side, as I do with my 100-year-old grandfather and 106-year-old great-grandmother, you may want to be more conservative with your withdrawals.

Retirement Spending

As you learned in chapter 12, you'll generally have two categories of expenses: fixed and variable. Fixed expenses tend to be the easier of the expense categories to figure out because you know they will be there each month. Variable expenses are typically those spent on the fun items in your budget, such as vacations, going out, hobbies, and gifts. There are also one-time expenses, which tend to be bigger-ticket items such as buying a new car, getting a new roof, or buying a sweet new motorized rascal scooter that makes the other retirees jealous.

The first step to income planning is to determine the amount of your fixed expenses. The goal of your retirement income plan may be to cover that amount with income from consistent nonmarket-based sources such as social security, pensions, and

129

annuities. In other words, if your fixed expenses were $4,000 a month, you may look to cover those expenses with a combination of social security, a pension, and/or an annuity. If you have a goal of taking a vacation each year, for example, you may want to consider covering that with a consistent income source to ensure you may take that vacation each year.

Next up is figuring out how to cover your variable expenses. This is where your withdrawal rate and strategy will come into play. Overall, a static withdrawal strategy, such as the 4% rule, means that you'll most likely leave too much money on the table if the market outperforms. Conversely, you may run out of money if the market underperforms. Is there a better withdrawal strategy?

Retirement income planning is a little like sailing. I've only gone sailing once, so I'm clearly an "expert" sailor. In sailing, your direction is constant, but you consistently deal with changing winds (stocks) and tides (inflation). To maintain the same direction, you adjust your sails to fit the environment. Withdrawal strategies should be looked at through the same lens. Just like you wouldn't point a boat in the direction you want to go and then make no adjustments along the way, you shouldn't keep your withdrawal strategy the same either. Using a dynamic withdrawal strategy may help you maintain a more stable income and could help maximize the overall value of your portfolio. Simply put, a dynamic withdrawal strategy means you take more income when the market is up and less income when the market is down.

GUARDRAILS

Dynamic withdrawal strategies are often referred to as "guardrail" or "floor and ceiling" strategies. They each have their slight differences, but the two concepts are similar. I'm going to focus on the guardrail approach. Guardrails are designed to help you determine when you should increase your withdrawals and when you should decrease them.

The first step is to set your initial withdrawal rate and adjust it each year by inflation. Next, your guardrails should be set at 20% above and 20% below your withdrawal rate. One bonus of the guardrail strategy is that you're required to set them for only 15 years. Once you get 15 years into retirement, the negative impacts of stock market drops have less of an impact moving forward. Table 26 provides a breakdown of the guardrail strategy.

Table 26. *Guardrail Strategy Outline*

	Portfolio Condition	**Withdrawal Adjustment**
Withdrawal Rule	When portfolio return is negative.	Don't adjust withdrawals for inflation. Keep spending flat.
Lower Guardrail	When the withdrawal rate increases by 20% more than the initial rate.	Reduce retirement spending by 10%.
Upper Guardrail	When the withdrawal rate decreases by 20% more than the initial rate.	Increase retirement spending by 10%.

Example

If you set your initial withdrawal rate at 5%, your upper guardrail will be 6% and your lower guardrail will be 4%. Let's look at sample numbers to explain this using a $1,000,000 account with a 5% withdrawal rate of $50,000 a year:

Portfolio Decrease

- If the value of your portfolio decreases to $800,000, your $50,000 withdrawal now becomes an unsustainable 6.25% withdrawal.
- The guardrail will tell you to reduce your withdrawal by 10%, so a $50,000 withdrawal now becomes $45,000.

Portfolio Increase

- If the value of your portfolio increases to $1,300,000, your $50,000 withdrawal now becomes a 3.85% withdrawal rate.
- You're free to increase your withdrawal by 10% and may take out $55,000 this year.

One item to note with the guardrail strategy is that although your withdrawal will drop by 10%, your take-home pay may not drop by that amount. If you were to take money from a qualified account for which withdrawals are taxed, you could reduce your taxable income. Table 27 provides some sample guardrails based on different withdrawal rates, and you may check out the website www.justreitrealready.com for a dynamic withdrawal worksheet.

Table 27. *Sample Guardrails*

Withdrawal Rate	Lower Guardrail	Upper Guardrail
3%	3.6%	2.4%
4%	4.8%	3.2%
5%	6%	4%

Overall, the goal of a dynamic withdrawal strategy is to seek to maximize the income from your retirement portfolio while working toward decreasing your risk of running out of money.

The guardrail strategy gives you the permission to enjoy more of your retirement. Vanguard conducted a study on dynamic withdrawal rates and found that "The more flexibility retirees have in the floor—the more they are able to reduce spending when the markets are performing poorly—the higher their potential success rate . . . Retirees' ability to accept changes in their floor helps their portfolio more than increasing their ceiling hurts it."[38] In other words, your ability to decrease spending during down markets will help keep your retirement portfolio healthy over the course of your retirement.

Chapter Highlights

- Since the mid-1990s, a "safe" withdrawal rate has been considered to be 4%.
- Many factors should go into determining your withdrawal rates:
  o Market returns
  o Non-portfolio income (e.g., social security, pension, annuities)
  o Inflation
  o Time horizon
- Dynamic withdrawals may provide an opportunity to take higher amounts in up markets and lower amounts in down markets.
- The guardrail strategy may help you set a guideline for when you should reduce your withdrawals and when you should increase them.
  o Guardrails are established with an initial withdrawal rate.

---

[38]   Colleen M. Jaconetti et al., "From Assets to Income: A Goals-Based Approach to Retirement Spending," Vanguard Research, April 2020, https://static.vg-content.info/crp/intl/gas/canada/documents/from-assets-to-income.pdf.

o The upper and lower guardrails represent a 20% decrease or 20% increase, respectively, in your withdrawal rate.

o If the guardrails you set are triggered, you could either increase or decrease your spending by 10%.

- Dynamic withdrawals are designed to help maximize the value of portfolios in retirement, be flexible for retirees, and potentially reduce the risk of running out of money during retirement.

CHAPTER 19

IT'S LIKE COLLEGE BUT FOR OLD PEOPLE AND WITH MORE PRUNES

Retirement Tool: Long-Term Care Coverage
Retirement Risk: Medical Expenses

Take a minute, close your eyes, and think about where you'd like to live in retirement. Are you on a beach, a lake, in your home, or in a city you've always wanted to live in, or are you in a nursing home? Wait, a nursing home? No one pictures themselves living in a nursing home during their golden years, but that doesn't mean it can't or won't happen to you.

When it comes to long-term care planning, the most common question I'm asked is, "How do I hide my money to qualify for Medicaid?" Is that what you really want? Once you decide to go the Medicaid route, you must maintain an exceptionally low asset amount (currently around $2,000 for an individual) and a low-income level ($2,742/month for individuals or $5,484/month for a couple).[39] More importantly,

---

[39] "Medicaid Eligibility: 2023 Income, Asset & Care Requirements for Nursing Homes and Long-Term Care," American Council on Aging, last modified November 22, 2022, https://www.medicaidplanningassistance.org/medicaid-eligibility/.

your medical care is now in the hands of the government. If that's what you want, you may gift assets into trusts, spend down your assets, potentially buy a Medicaid annuity, or even divorce your spouse, but you'd need to do that before the five-year look-back period. Be sure to visit www.justretirealready. com for the current numbers at the time of your retirement.

What are your options if you'd like to have more control over your care? If you'd prefer not to rely on Medicaid, you realistically have two choices: self-funding your care or passing the risk off to an insurance carrier. Let's explore both options and how to plan for each one.

SELF-FUNDING

Self-funding is a fancy way of saying you're going to pay for your care out of your own pocket. When it comes to long-term care in retirement, you need to be aware of the three levels: in-home care, assisted living, and nursing home care. Assisted living is the least expensive, followed by in-home care, and nursing home care is the most expensive.

Allow me to quote myself from earlier: "If you look at just the monthly national average cost of an in-home health aide in 2051 and project that over the average time long-term care is needed, a male would need $434,122 over 2.2 years to cover the cost, while a female would need $717,971 over 3.7 years." Wow, what a quote. All of this is to say that long-term care is and will be very costly.

If you'd like to self-fund your care, you're going to need to allocate hundreds of thousands of dollars toward long-term care. The solution for doing so is simple, but not easy. Your first option is to do nothing and hope you never get sick enough to need care. I'm not the biggest fan of that strategy, but it is an option. Your second option is to set aside a portion of your retirement assets for long-term care. For example, if you set aside $100,000 at the beginning of your retirement, kept it invested over 20 years, and potentially earn 6% per year, you'd have a pool of roughly $320,000 for long-term care. Alternatively, you'd have to save about $8,700 a year to reach the same $320,000 after 20 years.

When It Makes Sense to Self-Fund

Self-funding does have a couple of advantages. First, if you never get sick you may spend the funds or pass them on to your heirs. Second, there's no medical underwriting involved with a self-funding strategy. Generally, self-funding makes sense when you're at one of two ends of the asset spectrum: you have a little bit of money or more money than you could probably spend. When you have fewer assets, you may be able to self-fund for a little while, but usually the ultimate end game is to go on Medicaid. When you have an abundance of assets, you may usually afford to pay for the care outright and may not need the leverage that an insurance policy would provide.

Potential Drawbacks

Self-funding does require a large allocation of your assets that may be better served or used elsewhere. This may bring a level of uncertainty about possibly paying for a large expense throughout your retirement that may restrict your spending during your healthy years.

Self-funding your long-term care coverage may also mean losing out on the leverage provided by a long-term care insurance carrier. Long-term care policies could potentially provide significant coverage compared to the dollars you'd spend on premiums. They also offer an immediate benefit if you were to qualify for care. In a self-funding option, if you were to get sick early on in retirement or end up in a nursing home, you may not have the funds available to cover the cost.

LONG-TERM CARE INSURANCE

Passing off the risk of a long-term care event to a long-term care (LTC) insurance carrier is another option to consider. Since you're pooling long-term care risks with other people, you do get the benefit of leverage with an LTC policy.

There are two types of LTC insurance to assess: traditional and hybrid. Traditional LTC policies are designed to cover only a long-term care event. Hybrid policies include either a permanent life insurance policy from which you may access a portion of the death benefit for long-term care, or an LTC policy with a death benefit (or return of premium). Here's a breakdown of the two types of LTC policies.

Traditional Long-Term Care

LTC insurance is designed to give you an influx of cash in the event you have a long-term care event. LTC policies may be complicated, but there are three main items to consider: when the policy will pay a benefit, how much the benefit will pay, and how long the benefit will last.

When

- LTC insurance will pay a benefit to you if you can't perform two of the six activities of daily living: bathing, dressing, getting in and out of a bed or chair, walking, using the toilet, and eating. Most LTC policies will also pay benefits if there are cognitive issues such as Alzheimer's.

- Most LTC policies have a 90-day waiting period, which means you could potentially go 90 days without being able to perform activities of daily living before a carrier will start paying benefits.

How Much

- LTC policies provide a daily or monthly benefit, such as $200 a day.
- LTC policies provide a benefit for a number of years, such as three or five. The total benefit will be the value per day times the number of years, which is often referred to as a "pool of benefits." For example, if your daily benefit is $200 and you have a three-year benefit, your pool of benefits would be $219,000.
- Most LTC policies have an inflation rider, so the benefit will increase over time. The inflation rider will build up the benefit value before you use it, not during the claim. For example, if the inflation rider is 3%, a $200 daily benefit would grow to $268 after 10 years.
- Joint LTC policies may offer a shared pool of money as well.

How Long

- Most LTC policies have a benefit period with a set length of time, usually three to five years.
- LTC policies normally last until the pool of funds runs out, not the length of time.

LTC policies have several moving parts, but there are a variety of ways to customize the coverage to your needs and budget.

When It Makes Sense for an LTC Policy

LTC policies make sense for people who have a moderate amount of assets that wouldn't be able to fully fund a long-term care event on their own. LTC policies provide leverage by pooling risk together with thousands of other people. Essentially, you pay a premium you *may* afford to cover an event you *can't* afford. LTC policies also come with four additional benefits:

1. Some states have laws that will let a person exclude their house or a moderate amount of assets and still qualify for Medicaid.
2. They usually provide some level of help from a long-term care coordinator who may help you file the claim and find care that matches your needs.
3. They come with some tax benefits. Depending on your situation, you may be eligible to deduct premiums for an LTC policy. Also, though long-term care benefits aren't taxed, your self-funded account withdrawals may be. With an LTC policy, you may use a tax-free benefit to cover a long-term care expense if you're in a higher tax bracket, which may help significantly reduce your tax liability.
4. Some policies allow couples to pool their benefits. If one spouse gets sick, they may be able to access the benefit pool of the healthy spouse to help offset the cost of long-term care.

Potential Drawbacks

There are three potential drawbacks to LTC policies:

1. They are subject to medical underwriting, so you may not qualify for coverage even if you wanted it.

2. The rates aren't locked in, so you may experience premium increases over the life of the policy, making it difficult to budget for them.

3. If you never need care, then you've paid those premiums over the years but received no benefit.

Hybrid Long-Term Care

One question I'm often asked when it comes to long-term care is, "What happens if I never need it?" Like most other insurances, you should be happy that you never needed to file a claim, but if you don't use it, you lose it. You could pay premiums for years and never receive a benefit from owning the policy. That's where hybrid LTC policies come in.

With a hybrid LTC policy, you give the insurance carrier a lump sum or set number of payments, and they provide you with either long-term care coverage or a death benefit. Some permanent life insurance policies give you the ability to access a portion of your death benefit for long-term care coverage. The death benefit value may grow, or it may simply be a return of your original payment. The real cost of the policy is the opportunity cost of investing the funds elsewhere. Either way, you're paying a premium knowing that you'll either use it for long-term care expenses or receive a death benefit (more accurately your beneficiaries).

When It Makes Sense for a Hybrid LTC Policy

Hybrid LTC policies may be useful when you'd like to ensure that you're not "throwing your money away" on an insurance product you may never use. Hybrid policies also offer benefits that are similar to those of a traditional LTC policy, such as access to a care coordinator, preferential state laws, and potential tax benefits. Wealthier people typically use hybrid LTC policies for their tax benefits because the payments are tax free.

Potential Drawbacks

Some hybrid LTC policies will grow based on the performance of underlying investments, so there may be an element of investment risk built into the policy. In addition, unlike with a traditional life insurance policy, not all death benefits from a hybrid LTC policy are tax free. Since the long-term care rider on a permanent life insurance policy doesn't grow with inflation, it may ultimately be more cost effective to buy a regular LTC policy and then invest the difference.

Choosing a long-term care strategy to implement in retirement may be challenging, and there are definitely some nuances to understand before purchasing one. To help with this, I created table 28 to show you a hypothetical comparison of the three different strategies. Each is from the viewpoint of a 65-year-old male in standard health and assumes a 6% annual rate of return.

Table 28. *Comparing Long-Term Care Strategies*

Type of Strategy	Annual Cost	Total Cost	Initial LTC Coverage at Age 65	LTC Pool Coverage at Age 85
Self-Funded (Lump Sum)	N/A	$100,000	$100,000	$320,714
Self-Funded (Annual)	$8,700	$174,000	$8,700	$320,034
Traditional LTC	$2,523	$50,460	$186,150	$336,207
Hybrid LTC (Lump Sum)	N/A	$100,000	$304,916	$434,992
Hybrid LTC (Annual)	$10,000	$100,000	$111,030	$450,771

Source: Hypothetical illustrations generated using National Guardian Life's EssentialLTC planner and Lincoln Financial Group's MoneyGuard' solutions.

In this example, the lowest cost option would be to buy an LTC policy, but the hybrid policies offer more overall coverage. Based on these options, the hypothetical retiree may be able to whittle down their decision based on their current liquidity (i.e., whether they may afford a lump sum payment), the amount of coverage they'd like (none is an answer), and their current tax situation.

While you may not envision your retirement in a nursing home or with a caregiver in your home three times a week, you do need to acknowledge the possibility of that occurring. Frankly, we all know someone in our lives who has needed this type of care. We may look to prepare and plan, or we may avoid it until it becomes an issue. Preparing for a long-term care event may mean staying in your home longer or getting to choose your care facility over the government's predetermined one. Take control now, because you may not be able to take control later.

Chapter Highlights

- A long-term care event may potentially be very costly and may even severely impact your retirement.
- To mitigate the risk of a long-term care event, you may choose to self-fund or purchase an LTC or hybrid LTC policy.
- Self-funding your long-term care gives you the greatest liquidity and the ability to use the funds for any other purpose.
- LTC policies provide immediate leverage with a long-term care benefit and may potentially be a lower-cost option compared to other strategies.
- Hybrid LTC policies offer either a death benefit or long-term care coverage. Permanent life insurance policies offer riders that will let you access a portion of the

death benefit for long-term care, but there's no inflation protection on most of these riders.
- Deciding on your long-term care strategy may come
down to your liquidity, tax situation, and desire for
excess services.

CHAPTER 20

SOCIAL SECURITY—LIVING OFF THE GOVERNMENT

Retirement Tool: Social Security
Retirement Risks: Market, Sequence of Returns,
Inflation, Longevity

In the late '60s and early '70s, Stanford psychologist Walter Mischel conducted a study on delayed gratification using four- and five-year-olds as his subjects. You may have heard of it. It was called the marshmallow test. During the experiment, Mischel gave the kids an option: they could either have one marshmallow now or wait and have two when he came back into the room 15 minutes later. The goal of the study was to evaluate whether delayed gratification had predictive results on a child's future. Only about 30% of the kids were able to wait the full 15 minutes.[40] You may be thinking to yourself, *How could the kids not wait just 15 minutes?* Ultimately, there were

---

[40] Melissa Healy, "The Surprising Thing the 'Marshmallow Test' Reveals About Kids in an Instant-Gratification World," *Los Angeles Times, June 26, 2018, https://www.latimes.com/science/sciencenow/la-sci-sn-marshmallow-test-kids-20180626-story.html.*

some problems with this study, but the idea of delayed gratification applies to more than just children.

When given the choice, most retirees actively choose to take less income in retirement. Many retirees lack the patience or the ability to wait. Social security payments are designed to increase over time, however, so the earlier you take social security, the less income you'll receive. The earliest a retiree may take social security is at age 62, yet 41% of retirees choose to take social security at age 62 and over 50% take it before age 65.[41] Retirees are choosing one marshmallow over two. Let's look at how you may make the best decision to maximize your social security benefits.

To qualify for social security benefits, you need at least 40 quarters' worth of earnings (approximately 10 years). Your benefit is determined by two factors: your earnings history (which is based on the average of your 35 highest earning years) and the age you start taking benefits. You're eligible to take social security retirement benefits from age 62 to age 70. Your earnings will depend on your full retirement age (FRA), which the Social Security Administration determines based on the year you were born (see table 29). Think of your FRA as your baseline; it's the age when you'd start receiving your full benefits. If you wait to take your social security benefits until your FRA, you'll receive 100% of them. Conversely, each year you take benefits earlier, you'll see a reduction in your benefits.

---

[41] "Social Security: Five Things You Need to Know," Putnam Investments, PowerPoint, PPT200 328161 12/21, accessed May 16, 2022, https://www.putnam.com/literature/pdf/II937.pdf.

Table 29. *Social Security FRA Table*

Birth Year	FRA
1943–1954	66
1955	66 and 2 months
1956	66 and 4 months
1957	66 and 6 months
1958	66 and 8 months
1959	66 and 10 months
1960+	67

Source: "Plan for Retirement," Social Security Administration, accessed August 19, 2022, https://www.ssa.gov/prepare/plan-retirement.

Table 30 presents an example of a retiree born after 1960 with an FRA of 67 and an expected benefit of $24,000.

Table 30. *Example of Social Security Payouts Based on Age*

Age	Percentage of Full Retirement Benefit	Annual Benefit
62	70%	$16,800
63	75%	$18,000
64	80%	$19,200
65	86.7%	$20,798
66	93.3%	$22,399
67	100%	$24,000

Source: "Plan for Retirement," Social Security Administration.

Though taking benefits early ensures that you'll receive more social security payments, you'll get them at a reduced amount. Based on the example in table 30, taking benefits as early as possible means you'll reduce your income by 30%!

You may be thinking, *I know I'm getting less, but I'm getting five more years of payments by taking it early.* That's correct. Plus, if we factor in a 2% inflation rate, the breakeven point for waiting until FRA is age 81. By that age, if you had started taking the funds at 62, you'd have $408,196, and if you waited to start taking the funds until age 67, you'd have $415,042. If you project living longer than 81 years, it will most likely make more sense for you to wait to take social security. The "breakeven ages" typically run from age 81 to age 84.

Social security further incentivizes you to wait even longer to take benefits by increasing your payments 8% per year, from your FRA until age 70 (see table 31).

Table 31. *Example of How Social Security Payments Increase after FRA*

Age	Percentage of Full Retirement Benefit	Annual Benefit
67	100%	$24,000
68	108%	$25,920
69	116%	$27,840
70	124%	$29,760

Source: "Plan for Retirement," Social Security Administration.

In this example, waiting until age 70 would mean increasing your annual benefit by 24% from your FRA. Getting an 8% rate of return with no risk is nearly impossible in the market, but social security will give you that return for waiting. By comparison, the breakeven point when starting benefits between age 62 and 70 is age 82 ($433,160 vs. $436,887, respectively). This means that at age 82, your income would be

$24,964 if you started taking benefits at age 62 and $37,743 if you started taking benefits at age 70.

While the math may say to wait, you may find yourself in a position where you need to take income early. To make the best decision, ask yourself four questions:

1. **Do I need income right away?**

   Let's face it, not everyone is in the position to wait to take social security benefits. Often, people must retire much earlier than expected due to a layoff or an unexpected health event. The reality is that we may not be able to retire when we want to. If you fall into that category, you may want to consider taking social security benefits earlier.

2. **Am I still working?**

   You may want to be careful if you're working and would like to collect benefits before your FRA. Social security will offset your benefits if you're still working and collecting benefits. If you're under your FRA, social security will offset your benefits by $1 for every $2 of earnings you have over their annual limit and offset your benefits by $1 for every $3 of earnings in the year of your FRA. Generally, even if you have modest earnings, your benefits could be subject to an offset. Once you hit your FRA, you may make as much money as you want, and social security will not offset or reduce your benefits.

3. **Do I have any tax considerations?**

   Ugh, there he goes with taxes again. Social security benefits are counted as income and could push you up into another tax bracket and/or impact the cost of your Medicare premiums. It will be important for you to consider the tax implications of taking social security payments. Most retirees have a short window to make Roth conversions in retirement, and taking social security payments earlier may close that window.

4. **What is my life expectancy?**
I know that no one knows for sure when they will die, but we may take an educated guess based on a few factors. In this instance, it helps to think like a life insurance carrier. If you think they'd love to insure you because you're so healthy, you may want to consider delaying benefits. If you have a family history of longevity, it may make sense to delay benefits, and vice versa. If you're overweight, don't eat healthy, and/or smoke cigarettes, you may want to take benefits early.

All these questions are to illustrate that as much as financial experts may like it to be, retirement planning isn't just about math. It's deeply personal, and a decision like taking social security should be based on your individual situation. Advisors may show you that if you live past a certain age it makes sense to wait, but you may not be able to, and that's fine. Your aim should be to maximize your income from social security. Go get as many marshmallows as you may.

How To Maximize Your Social Security Benefits If You're Married

Spouses who've been married for at least one year are entitled to their own benefit or 50% of their spouse's social security benefit (if they wait until their own FRA to collect), whichever is greater. In some cases, such as when both spouses have somewhat equal earnings over their lifetime, 50% of one spouse's benefit will be less than the earnings of the other, so that spouse would collect their own benefit.

Alternatively, there may be a decent differential earnings history between spouses. If you're the higher-income spouse, your spouse would most likely look to collect 50% of your social security benefit. For example, if your FRA monthly benefit is $2,400 and your spouse's FRA monthly benefit is $500, your spouse would be able to collect $1,200 a month. Basically, your spouse would be eligible for an extra $700 a month if they collected 50% of your benefit.

Spouses are eligible to collect the spousal benefit as early as age 62, but their benefit will be reduced each year they are under their FRA. Table 32 illustrates what this would look like using the same $2,400 monthly benefit and assuming you're the higher-income-earning spouse.

Table 32. *Social Security Spousal Benefits*

Your Spouse's Age	Percentage of Your Full Benefit	Annual Benefit
62	32.5%	$7,800
63	35%	$8,400
64	37.5%	$9,000
65	41.7%	$10,008
66	45.8%	$10,992
67	50%	$12,000

Source: "Plan for Retirement," Social Security Administration.

In addition, spousal benefits may be reduced based on the collecting spouse's age. As you might notice, benefits are reduced each year that falls earlier than your established FRA (as much as 32.5% at age 62). It doesn't matter when you decide to take benefits, it only matters when your spouse decides to take benefits. Table 33 depicts four scenarios.

Table 33. *Social Security Spousal Benefit Examples*

	You Claim at Age 62	You Claim at Age 67 (Your FRA)
Your Spouse Claims at Age 62	Your benefit: $1,680 Your spouse's benefit: $780	Your benefit: $2,400 Your spouse's benefit: $780
Your Spouse Claims at Age 67 (their FRA)	Your benefit: $1,680 Your spouse's benefit: $1,200	Your benefit: $2,400 Your spouse's benefit: $1,200

Spousal benefits are always based on two things: the higher-income spouse's benefit at their FRA and the age they start collecting social security. Spousal benefits are not impacted if the higher-income spouse starts taking social security early. In this scenario, if your spouse starts collecting at age 62, their monthly benefit drops from $1,200 to $780. Their benefit isn't impacted by when you collect social security.

You may maximize your spousal benefits by ensuring that you're collecting the highest total monthly benefit. For some couples that may mean collecting their individual benefits. For others that may mean collecting one spouse's benefit along with half of the other's. As an FYI, a spouse may collect the spousal benefit even if they don't have a full earnings history.

HOW TO MAXIMIZE YOUR SOCIAL SECURITY BENEFITS IF YOU'RE A DIVORCED SPOUSE

There are some perks to being divorced. Social security will let a retiree collect on their divorced spouse's benefit if they were married for at least 10 years, have been divorced for two years, and are at least age 62 (60 if disabled). The ex-spouse must also be age 62 for you to collect. They don't need to file, and it doesn't matter if they remarry.

If you remarry before age 50, you forfeit your ex-spouse's benefit, but if you remarry after age 60, you're still eligible for your ex-spouse's benefit if it's higher than your current spouse's benefit. Unfortunately, you can't collect on more than one spouse/ex-spouse's benefit, though I'm sure some people have tried.

Other than that, divorced spouses are subject to the same rules as married spouses. They may collect up to 50% of their ex-spouse's benefits if they collect at FRA. Benefits will be reduced by the same percentage as a married couple.

SURVIVOR BENEFITS

Survivor benefits work differently for divorced spouses and married couples. A survivor is allowed to collect on either their own social security benefit or their deceased spouse's benefit, but not both at the same time. To collect a survivor benefit, you must meet the following requirements:

- You must have been married for at least 10 years.
- You can't remarry before age 60.
- You must be at least age 60 to start collecting (age 50 if you're disabled). You may collect benefits early if you're caring for children under the age of 16.

You may notice that a surviving spouse is eligible to collect survivor benefits two years earlier than they may collect in any other scenario. Not surprisingly, the benefits are reduced each year before the surviving spouse reaches their FRA. Table 34 provides a breakdown of a scenario based on a $24,000 annual benefit with an FRA of 67.

Table 34. *Survivor Social Security Benefit Reduction Schedule*

Surviving Spouse	Percentage of Full Survivor Benefit	Annual Benefit
60	71.5%	$17,160
61	75.6%	$18,144
62	79.6%	$19,104
63	83.7%	$20,088
64	87.8%	$21,072
65	91.9%	$22,056
66	95.9%	$23,016
67	100%	$24,000

Source: "Plan for Retirement," Social Security Administration.

Survivor benefits do have one advantage compared to the other social security scenarios: you're allowed to collect one benefit and then switch to the other. For example, you may start collecting the survivor benefit at age 60, let your own benefit increase until age 70, then switch to your own social security benefit at age 70.

There are numerous iterations you may evaluate, but spouses will fall into one of three categories: the deceased spouse has a higher FRA, the surviving spouse has a higher FRA, or both spouses have about the same FRA. Here are two scenarios to evaluate (I used no inflation for these numbers):

1. **The Deceased Spouse Has a Higher FRA**
   Deceased spouse's annual FRA benefit = $24,000
   Surviving spouse's annual FRA benefit = $12,000
   When the deceased spouse had the higher FRA benefit, there are three collection options that will help maximize your income from social security depending on when you need income (see figure 20 for a comparison and breakeven ages):

   Option 1: Collect the survivor benefit as early as possible.
   - Collecting the survivor benefit at age 60 would mean receiving $1,430 a month, or $17,160 per year.
   - By the end of age 85, you'd have collected $446,160.
   - With this option, you get to collect benefits two years earlier than you would if you collected your own.
   - This option makes sense when you may have a shorter life expectancy, need income earlier, and/or don't have tax concerns.

   Option 2: Collect your benefit at 62, then switch to the survivor benefit at 65.
   - Collecting your benefits at age 62 would mean receiving $796 a month, or $9,552 per year.
   - At age 65, you may then switch to your survivor benefit, which is $1,838 a month, or $22,056 a year (91.9% of their FRA).
   - By the end of age 85, you'd have collected $491,832.
   - This option still allows you to collect income early and may line up better if you decide to retire at age 65.

- You'll have to consider how other income (e.g., if you're still working) may offset your early social security income.

Option 3: Collect your benefit at 62, then switch to the survivor benefit at your FRA.

- Collecting your benefits at age 62 would mean receiving a benefit of $796 a month, or $9,552 per year.
- At age 67, you may then switch to the survivor benefit, which would be $2,000 a month, or $24,000 a year.
- By end of age 85, you'd have collected $503,760.
- This option still allows you to collect income early, and it may provide you with the most long-term income.
- You'll have to consider how other income (e.g., if you're still working) may offset your early social security income.

Figure 20: Breakeven Points for Deceased Spouse Scenarios w/ Higher FRA. This scenario was created by the Author, Derek Mazzarella, CFP.

2. **The Deceased Spouse Has a Lower FRA**

Deceased spouse's annual FRA benefit = $12,000

Surviving spouse's annual FRA benefit = $24,000

When the deceased spouse had a lower FRA benefit, the surviving spouse has a little more flexibility with when they choose to take social security benefits. Ultimately, in almost every scenario, it makes sense to take the survivor benefits first and then collect on your benefit. Here are three different options to consider (see figure 21 for a comparison and breakeven ages):

Option 1: Collect the survivor benefit at 60, then switch to yours at your FRA.

- Collecting the survivor benefit starting at age 60 would mean receiving $715 a month, or $8,580 per year.
- At age 67, you may switch to your benefit and collect $2,000 a month, or $24,000 a year.
- By the end of age 85, you'd have collected $516,060.
- With this option, you get to collect benefits at age 60 and then get a pay bump at age 67.
- This option makes sense when you may have a shorter life expectancy, need income earlier, and/or don't have tax concerns.

Option 2: Collect the survivor benefit at 65, then switch to yours at 70.

- Collecting the survivor benefit at age 65 would mean receiving $919 a month, or $11,028 per year.
- At age 70, you may switch to your benefit and collect $2,480 a month, or $29,760 a year.
- By the end of age 85, you'd have collected $531,300.

157

- This option would line up with a retirement age of 65. You'd be able to increase the survivor benefit by waiting, and you may avoid or offset tax concerns.
- With this option, you wouldn't be able to collect benefits earlier, so it may not make sense for those who may have shorter life expectancies.

Option 3: Collect the survivor benefit at 60, then switch to yours at 70.

- Collecting the survivor benefit at age 60 would mean receiving $715 a month, or $8,580 per year.
- At age 70, you may then switch to your benefit and collect $2,480 a month, or $29,760 a year.
- By end of age 85, you'd have collected $561,960.
- This option may give you the most long-term income overall.
- With this option, you may have tax issues and benefit offsets that would reduce the value of your social security income.

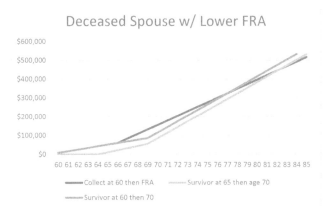

Deceased Spouse w/ Lower FRA

Figure 21: Breakeven Points for Deceased Spouse Scenarios w/ Lower FRA. This scenario was created by the Author, Derek Mazzarella, CFP.

If you and your deceased spouse had wages that were relatively similar, you may want to take the deceased spouse's benefits first, then push back collecting your own benefits until age 70. It's up to you to figure out the right timing, but you may use this as a general guide.

Chapter Highlights

- Social security benefits are based on your earnings record (the average of your 35 highest earning years) and when you decide to start taking your benefits.
- Your full retirement age (FRA) is based on your date of birth.
- Many retirees start taking social security before their FRA, and an overwhelming majority of those take benefits at age 62.
- Taking benefits before your FRA can reduce your benefits, and delaying them after your FRA may potentially increase your benefits.
- There are four questions you should ask yourself before deciding when to start taking social security:
  1. Do I need income right away?
  2. Am I still working?
  3. Do I have any tax considerations?
  4. What is my life expectancy?
- Spouses are eligible to collect on half of the other spouse's benefit if it's more than their own.
- Divorced spouses may collect on half of their ex-spouse's benefit if the benefit is more than their own. They must have been married for 10 years, be divorced for two, and be 62 or older.
- Widowed/widowered spouses may collect either their own benefit or their deceased spouse's benefit, and surviving spouses may collect one benefit then switch to the other benefit at a later date.

CHAPTER 21

THE RETIREMENT TOOLBOX

I f you've reached this point, you've just absorbed a lot of information, numbers, and data from tables and figures. We reviewed ten different retirement tools, seven of which can cover or mitigate more than one retirement risk. Some tools are well known, such as social security, LTC insurance, and annuities. You may have even considered implementing some of these tools already. Other tools may seem foreign to you. Hopefully, in either case, I've given you a few different thoughts on how to implement each tool or strategy.

If you need a quick reference guide, table 35 provides a breakdown of the seven retirement risks and which retirement tools may combat them.

Table 35. *Retirement Tool Matrix*

Retirement Tool	Market Risk	Sequence of Returns	Health-care	Infla-tion	Taxes	Lon-gevity	Death in Retirement
Diversification	X	X		X			
Bucket Strategy	X	X		X		X	
Permanent Life Insurance	X	X	X		X		X
Annuities	X	X			X	X	
Asset Location					X		
Withdrawal Sequence					X		
Dynamic Withdrawals	X	X		X			
Long-Term Care			X				
Reverse Mortgage	X	X			X	X	
Social Security	X	X		X		X	

*This is a hypothetical example and is not representative of any specific situation, your results will vary.

Revisit the assessment questions outlined in chapter 10 and see how you'd answer them now. Has anything changed with your approach? What tool or strategy would make the most impact for you? What resonated with you the most and why? What's something you could implement rather seamlessly, and what's something you would need some help with? If you do need help, go get it. Pause and take some notes next to your answers.

As you're answering those questions, keep in mind that retirement planning is thought to be mainly numbers-focused, but there *is* an emotional side of retirement as well. How would removing or reducing these risks make you feel? How would you feel if you ended up doing nothing and one of these risks negatively impacts your retirement?

The ultimate goal of this book is to help you enjoy your retirement to the fullest, whatever that looks for you. While these retirement tools may help you raise your retirement potential success rate, they're also meant to help you enjoy more of your retirement. You'll be able to focus on the things that matter to you because you won't be thinking about the next market crash or worrying about whether your money will last. If your tax bill were lower and you were able to generate more income, what would you be able to do that you didn't think was possible?

While we've discussed each tool at length, it may be hard to see how they'd fit into your life and retirement. To tie this all together, I'm going to compare the retirements of two different retirees. With their respective stories, I'll take you through the most common stages of retirement so you may see how the various retirement risks will present themselves. Notice how each retiree's retirement toolbox is equipped or unequipped to handle each stage and risk.

Keep in mind both retirees are starting their retirement at the same age, begin with the same amount of assets, have the same income needs, and will live for the same amount of time. One retiree follows conventional planning, while the other retiree implements an array of retirement tools that I've outlined in this book. Do you see yourself as either one of these retirees? Think about which one you'd rather be and how you'd feel in either situation. These stories also illustrate that it doesn't always take making drastic changes to see significant results.

CHAPTER 22

A TALE OF TWO RETIREMENTS

W hile numbers are one thing and are often what we advisors focus on, the most meaningful result is how clients feel after working with us. They've told me they feel lighter and more confident in their future. Let's look at those two hypothetical retirement stories, and as you're reading, think about which retiree feels more confident and lighter.

SAM

Sam is very smart and knowledgeable, and he often reads about finances. He has invested in low-cost index funds (annuities are too expensive), bought term insurance and invested the difference, saved diligently into his employer's 401(k) plan on a pre-tax basis, and paid down his mortgage as fast as possible. Sam has an investment account, and the bond portion of his portfolio is invested in municipal bonds for tax-free income. He has saved enough in the 401(k) plan to be a millionaire, so he doesn't have any debt heading into retirement and may cover 70% of his pre-tax earnings (since that's what the financial professionals said retirees need). At age 65, Sam is now tired of the rat race and ready to retire.

In the run-up before Sam's retirement, the stock market had done well, so he had no reason to believe that the market wouldn't continue to do so. Still, Sam decides to de-risk his retirement portfolio and pick a traditional 60/40 portfolio asset mix. He withdraws 4% per year, believing that the money will last 30 years. Add his social security benefits to the mix, and Sam's outlook is good. He's taking social security a couple of years early, but the drop in income shouldn't matter much considering he's collecting two more years of payments.

The first six months of Sam's first year of retirement, the market that was doing so well drops by over 20%. Only 60% of his portfolio was in stocks, but he still doesn't feel good seeing his account that was once over $1,000,000 drop to below $900,000. While Sam wants to keep true to the 4% rule, his expenses haven't changed and he still needs to take out the same dollar amount. Sam gets a little nervous and moves some money to cash.

Two years later, the market rebounds and reaches new all-time highs. Sam's portfolio isn't what it once was, but at least it's still producing enough income. A few years after that, he experiences some issues with his house and needs to take out extra money for repairs. His portfolio takes another hit, but he knows that if any adjustments must be made, he may make them later; it's still time to enjoy his retirement.

Flash forward, and Sam has reached the age when he needs to take RMDs. Once he figures out how much he needs to withdraw, he realizes it's more than the "safe" withdrawal rate. Sam ends up taking out more than he needs, but he figures he may just reinvest it into his investment account. Unfortunately, because of the extra income from his RMDs, Sam's taxes and Medicare premiums increase, which moves him up to the next Medicare income bracket.

Now Sam's health is slowly getting worse, and he needs to spend more money on his medical expenses that are increasing at higher inflation rates than normal. As Sam gets older, his portfolio shrinks at a faster rate than expected. The stock market sees more 20%+ drops, his medical bills are adding up, and he's getting nervous. He starts counting every dollar, going out less, and cutting lifestyle expenses.

Despite his health issues, Sam is living longer than expected, so his medical bills are adding up. His kids live in another state and are pushing for in-home nursing care, which eventually Sam reluctantly agrees to. He never purchased LTC insurance because he thought it was a waste of money.

The once robust retirement portfolio Sam had is now on its last legs, and eventually Sam must drain all the money out of his account. Medicaid is within his sight, but it's not what he had thought was in store for his retirement. He constantly thinks about what he should've done differently. He followed every financial rule that conventional wisdom says is the right thing to do and wonders where he went wrong.

PAT

Pat has the same starting point as Sam. She's the same age, has the same income, saves the same amount into the same types of accounts, and retires at the same time. Going into retirement, Pat makes a few changes compared to Sam. She decides to put a portion of her 401(k) plan into a variable annuity that will pay a lifetime income, and she begins taking that income at age 65. Pat diversifies her investment portfolio by segmenting it into buckets based on time horizons. After running the numbers, she decides that waiting until age 70 to take social security would be best.

A year into Pat's retirement, the market drops by over 20%. Pat is nervous at first, but she realizes she already has two years' worth of cash to pull from. She's going to let her mid-term and long-term buckets recover before making any shifts. Plus, she's already withdrawing some income from her annuity, and that income isn't impacted by the market. Pat doesn't make any changes and continues to enjoy her retirement.

Two years later, the market has rebounded and Pat's in good shape. Since she's using a dynamic withdrawal strategy, she may take excess returns from her portfolio. She uses those excess withdrawals to take up a new hobby. After a few years go by, Pat's house needs some repairs. Since her portfolio has been holding solid and she kept her emergency fund fully funded, Pat pulls from her emergency fund to make the repairs. Her retirement portfolio remains intact.

Flash forward, and Pat has now reached RMD age. Once she figures out how much she needs to withdraw, she realizes it's minimal. Since she delayed taking social security and withdrew from her investment account in the first few years of her retirement, Pat used that time to convert some of her traditional 401(k) funds to Roth funds. Her tax bill stayed relatively the same, and her Medicare premiums remained in the lowest income bracket.

Now Pat's health is slowly getting worse, and she needs to spend more money on the medical expenses that are increasing at higher inflation rates than normal. The stock market sees more 20%+ drops and her medical bills are adding up, but Pat has been adjusting her withdrawals along with the market. Her portfolio is still in good shape, and her social security payments and annuity are covering her essential fixed expenses. Pat knows that no matter what happens, the essentials are covered.

Despite her health issues, Pat is living longer than expected, so her medical bills are adding up. Pat's kids live in another state and are pushing for in-home nursing care, which eventually Pat reluctantly agrees to. Though she was always annoyed by the payments, Pam had purchased LTC insurance before retiring, so the policy benefits are providing the funds to cover most of the costs of in-home care.

As Pat reflects on her retirement, she realizes how fortunate she was. Her foresight to plan, anticipate challenges, and integrate several types of retirement strategies helped her live retirement under her terms. If she was stressed at any point in retirement, it wasn't because of money. She always knew she had enough.

COMPARISON

Pat experienced the same issues as Sam in retirement, but Pat was prepared with a variety of financial tools. As a result, Pat's retirement was better positioned to handle the risks that may derail a retirement, whether that's market risk, inflation, healthcare, or taxes. Sam only had a couple of retirement tools available. When something unexpected happened, his retirement wasn't flexible enough to adjust. Sam's adjustment was to reduce his lifestyle expenses and rely on the government, which, in my opinion, is the last thing he should've done.

Comparing Sam's and Pat's retirements using my planning software, I was able to illustrate how their retirement strategies were suited to handle the different retirement risks. To do this, I used the same age, income, time horizon, and retirement/investment account balances for both retirees (see figures 22 and 23 and table 36).

Sam's Retirement

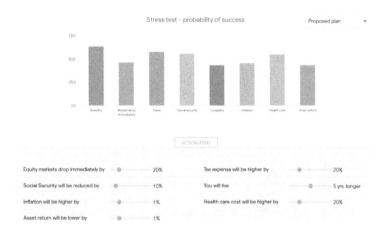

Figure 22: Sam's Stress Test and Probability of Success. Image generated using RightCapital Financial Planning Software. This is a hypothetical example and is not representative of any specific situation, your results will vary. The hypothetical rates of return do not reflect the deduction of fees and charges inherent to investing.

Unlike Sam, Pat made the following changes:

- Diversified her portfolio (compared to a 60% S&P and 40% bond index funds)
- Utilized a dynamic withdrawal strategy (guardrail)
- Converted $150,000 of her 401(k) to a qualified variable annuity with a 6% annual income benefit
- Converted qualified funds to a Roth IRA
- Waited until age 70 to take social security
- Purchased an LTC policy with a premium of $3,000 a year, a $170 daily benefit, and 3% compound inflation

Pat's Retirement

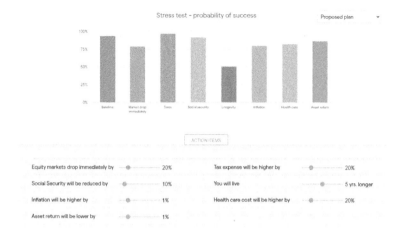

Equity markets drop immediately by — 20%   Tax expense will be higher by — 20%

Social Security will be reduced by — 10%   You will live — 5 yrs. longer

Inflation will be higher by — 1%   Health care cost will be higher by — 20%

Asset return will be lower by — 1%

Figure 23: Pat's Stress Test and Probability of Success. Image generated using RightCapital Financial Planning Software. This is a hypothetical example and is not representative of any specific situation, your results will vary. The hypothetical rates of return do not reflect the deduction of fees and charges inherent to investing.

Table 36. *Pat and Sam's Probability of Success Comparison*

Retirement Stress	Sam's Probability of Success	Pat's Probability of Success
Baseline (Normal Retirement)	63.5%	93.2%
Market Drop Immediately	46.2%	79%
Taxes	57.6%	96.5%
Social Security	55.6%	91.4%
Longevity	43.3%	50.5%
Inflation	45.8%	79.9%
Healthcare	54.8%	82.1%
Asset Return (Market Risk)	43.3%	86.3%

This is a hypothetical example and is not representative of any specific situation, your results will vary. The hypothetical rates of return do not reflect the deduction of fees and charges inherent to investing.

As you may see from the numbers and data, Pat's retirement was more resilient than Sam's retirement. They each started with the same amount of money with the same type of tax treatment, they were both the same age and had the same earnings, they retired at the same time, and they both had the same retirement planning horizon. Pat didn't save more money than Sam, but her retirement had a higher floor.

Ultimately, which retirement would you rather have? Do you want one that prepares you for a multitude of scenarios and risks or one that's reactionary? Which retirement would be more stressful? Which retirement would be more enjoyable?

CHAPTER 23

I LOVE IT WHEN A PLAN COMES TOGETHER

Well, we've been on quite a journey together and I'm sad that it's coming to an end. You, on the other hand, may be relieved. I started out with some depressing information about the state of retirement and then discussed seven risks that may derail your retirement. You had to know I wasn't going to leave it like that. We discussed 10 retirement tools that will help you create the retirement you're meant to have and then applied them to the retirement journeys of our two friends Sam and Pat.

Moving forward, you'll have to figure out which of these tools and strategies are right for you. For some people, life insurance won't be an option but an annuity would be. A reverse mortgage may not work for one person, but it could be critical for someone else. Realistically, financial planning is mostly math. If you're objective and run the numbers, you'll find out what will work best for you.

In order to help you extract value from this book, I've outlined an action plan for you to use as a guideline. Simply reading this book may give you a small sense of accomplishment, but you need to take action for your time to be worthwhile. Retirement may seem like a daunting task, but you may have a successful retirement by breaking your retirement down into simple actionable steps.

Retirement Action Plan

There's a wealth of information in this book and several different paths you may take to create an enjoyable retirement potentially free of financial stress. This information may feel overwhelming to you, but I want to make sure you have an action plan moving forward. I've outlined some broad steps to help get you started and give you an idea of what to implement for your own retirement.

1. **Establish Your Financial Priorities**

   When you take a vacation, you don't get in the car and start driving with the hope that you'll end up some place nice. You decide where you want to go. You should approach financial planning the same way. What do you want your retirement to look like? Are you working part time? Are you traveling? Where are you going to live? Are you volunteering? Are you watching the grandkids? Sit down and write out your financial priorities. How will you give your retirement meaning? What legacy would you like to leave?

2. **Get Organized**

   The next step I take with my clients is to get them organized. Most people have their assets in different places, aren't fully aware of their spending habits, and/or don't know their tax rates. Assess where you are financially and then determine a baseline for your net worth, tax bracket, wills and/or estate documents, insurance coverage, and so on, using a financial tool that aggregates your accounts in one place. If you don't like any of them, use an Excel spreadsheet.

3. **Determine Your Expenses**

   Your expenses set your baseline for retirement. They're your driving force between many of the decisions you'll make in retirement planning. Break down your expenses into fixed and variable. As a reminder, your fixed expenses are the expenses you expect to incur each month, such as your real estate taxes, Medicare payments, groceries, and utilities. Variable expenses are the ones that will change monthly. A good way to capture your variable expenses is to download a report from your credit card. Be sure to also account for one-time expenses.

4. **Evaluate Your Income Sources**

   Once you have your expenses figured out, the next step is to determine how much consistent income you'll be able to generate. Your goal should be to cover at least your fixed expenses with consistent income sources. For example, if social security covers 70% of your fixed expenses, you may look to fill the gap with an annuity or income from an insurance policy. Figure out whichever one makes the most sense for you.

5. **Use a Bucket Strategy**

   Segment your retirement funds into their respective buckets based on covering your variable income. As a reminder, put two years' worth of variable expenses into the cash bucket, three to five years' worth of expenses in the mid-term bucket, and the rest in the long-term bucket.

6. **Establish a Distribution Strategy**

   Your distribution strategy should include implementing the guardrail strategy along with determining the most tax-efficient withdrawal sequence. Be sure to pay attention to your tax bracket and when you may be close to hitting the next one. Remember, tax planning is a long-term game in which you should balance today with tomorrow.

7. **Consider LTC Coverage**

   Though you may not like thinking about it, you should consider the best course of action for you and your family in the event you'll need some form of LTC coverage. Are you planning on self-funding, or are you going to pass the risk off to an insurance carrier? If you're going for the latter, are you going to use a hybrid policy or a traditional LTC policy?

8. **Think about Estate Planning**

   I didn't mention estate planning in this book so far because it could be the topic of its own book. At minimum you should have a will, healthcare proxy, and power of attorney in place. If you already have them in place but haven't had them reviewed, be sure to do so, especially if you plan on moving to a different state. If you have assets that don't have a beneficiary already attached to them, such as a house or an investment account, consider setting up a trust to capture all of your non-beneficiary assets to avoid probate and ensure your assets go where you want them to.

The biggest challenge for you is what lies next, so put these tools to work for you. I've read dozens of self-help and business books over the years, and while most of them contained very useful information, they had one problem: me. I'd get into the habit of reading these books and thinking about how much sense they made, and though I might've implemented a few ideas here or there, I wasn't consistent. This book is designed to be a resource. You should be able to step into any chapter and pull ideas from it. Ultimately, it's on you to implement the strategies that you think would be the best fit for you. I can't do it for you. Also, make sure you check out the website www. justretirealready.com for additional tools and resources.

Here's to a healthy, wealthy, and fulfilled retirement!

LEAP FOR EDUCATION

LEAP for Education has a mission to empower underserved youth to achieve social and economic mobility by cultivating personal, educational, and career growth. LEAP students who can start with us as early as 6th grade, enroll in college at 2x the average rate for low-income students in Massachusetts and graduate at 4x the state average.

In 2023, LEAP served over six hundred youth in Lynn, Peabody, and Salem, three gateway cities about 10 miles north of Boston. LEAP's programs empower students from middle school through post-secondary graduation using a youth success model that includes academics, social-emotional learning, education and career readiness, and development of social capital.

LEAP's goal is to close the opportunity gap for its students who are predominantly low income and first-generation-to-college. We do this by:

1. offering project-based learning to help students explore multiple interests;
2. partnering with the business community who provide our students with career mentors and role models;
3. exposing students to different workplaces and cultural opportunities

4. helping each student create, and execute on, an education and career plan that is unique to them; and,
5. providing students with many trusted adults who support them and their families.

Interested to learn more? Visit us at www.leap4ed.org.

ACKNOWLEDGMENTS

Writing a book is not a one-person endeavor. This book grew from an idea in my head to thoughts on paper to an actual book with the help of several people. Realizing what I was good at and what I needed help with pushed this book over the finish line.

I'd like to relay my appreciation for the people that took the time to read my very rough first few drafts and gave me valuable feedback: my brother, Brian Mazzarella, my amazing client Barbara Wilson-Arboleda, and my colleague, Trish Sauer.

Thank you to all of those of you who chose to endorse this book. I'm forever grateful for your belief in me and this book.

To my marketing team, Silvi and Chris, thank you for always helping me make my visions a reality, no matter how challenging they may seem.

I want to recognize the work that my editor, Nancy Graham-Tillman, contributed to this book. Her work was, chef's kiss, excellent. Somehow, she turned a non-writer into an author and made it appear as if I had any ability to write. Every one of her ideas and notes improved this book.

This book would not have been possible without all the resources I was able to cite and incorporate into my financial planning process. Thank you to those other advisors and financial researchers that put the work in to help people have better retirements.

I want to recognize my publisher, Publish Your Purpose, for guiding a total novice through the publishing process and turning this book into a reality.

Finally, I want to thank my parents. To my mom who is always supportive, positive, caring, and my biggest fan. While my father is no longer with us, the lessons he taught me about hard work, being kind to other people, and making sure I have fun will last with me throughout the rest of my life.

BIBLIOGRAPHY

American Council on Aging. "Medicaid Eligibility: 2023 Income, Asset & Care Requirements for Nursing Homes and Long-Term Care." Last modified November 22, 2022. https://www.medicaidplanningassistance.org/medicaid-eligibility/.

Bengen, William P. "Determining Withdrawal Rates Using Historical Data." *Journal of Financial Planning*, October 1994, 171–180. https://www.retailinvestor.org/pdf/Bengen1.pdf.

Benz, Christine, Jefferey Ptak, and John Rekenthaler. "The State of Retirement Income: 2022, A Look at How Higher Bond Yields, Lower Equity Valuations, and Inflation Affect Starting Safe Withdrawal Rates." Morningstar. December 12, 2022. https://assets.contentstack.io/v3/assets/blt4eb-669caa7dc65b2/blt0cdaf6ab25075b47/6398c339313cec5f8f3b5c8a/The_State_Of_Retirement_Income_2022.pdf.

Benz, Christine, Jeffrey Ptak, and John Rekenthaler. "The State of Retirement Income: Safe Withdrawal Rates." Morningstar, November 11, 2021. https://www.morningstar.com/content/dam/marketing/shared/pdfs/Research/state-of-retirement-income.pdf.

Capital Group | American Funds. "What Past Stock Market Declines May Teach Us." Accessed May 27, 2022. https://

www.capitalgroup.com/individual/planning/market-fluc-tuations/past-market-declines.html.

Centers for Medicare and Medicaid. "2023 Medicare Costs." Accessed March 8, 2022. https://www.medicare.gov/Pubs/pdf/11579-medicare-costs.pdf.

Chen, Anqi, and Alicia H. Munnell. "How Much Taxes Will Retirees Owe on Their Income?" *Center for Retirement Research at Boston College*, no. 20-16 (January 2021). https://crr.bc.edu/wp-content/uploads/2020/12/IB_20-16_.pdf.

Davidson, Liz. "The History of Retirement Benefits." Workforce. June 21, 2016. https://workforce.com/news/the-history-of-retirement-benefits.

GBS Life Insurance. "Whole Life Dividend Rate History: 1995 to 2020." Accessed July 11, 2022. https://www.gbslife.com/media/29249/dividend-rate-report-2020.pdf.

Georgetown University Law Center. "A Timeline of the Evolution of Retirement in the United States." Workplace Flexibility 2010 Memos and Fact Sheets 50. March 26, 2010. https://scholarship.law.georgetown.edu/legal/50/.

Healy, Melissa. "The Surprising Thing the 'Marshmallow Test' Reveals about Kids in an Instant-Gratification World." *Los Angeles Times*, June 26, 2018. https://www.latimes.com/science/sciencenow/la-sci-sn-marshmallow-test-kids-20180626-story.html.

Ibbotson, Roger G. "Fixed Indexed Annuities: Consider the Alternatives." Zebra Capital Management & Yale School of Finance. January 2018. https://www.zebracapital.com/wp-content/uploads/2019/06/Fixed-Indexed-Annuities-Consider-the-Alternative-January-2018.pdf.

J. P. Morgan Asset Management. "Guide to the Markets." Last modified December 31, 2022. https://am.jpmorgan.com/content/dam/jpm-am-aem/global/en/insights/market-insights/guide-to-the-markets/mi-guide-to-the-markets-us.pdf.

Jaconetti, Colleen M., Michael A. DiJoseph, Francis M. Kinniry Jr., David Pakula, and Hank Lobel. "From Assets to Income: A Goals-Based Approach to Retirement Spending." Vanguard Research. April 2020. https://corporate.vanguard.com/content/dam/corp/research/pdf/from-assets-to-income-a-goals-based-approach-to-retirement-spending-usa-isgelr_042020_online.pdf.

Jurwitz, Mitchell, and John Levenstein, writers. *Arrested Development.* Season 1, episode 2, "Top Banana." Directed by Anthony Russo, featuring Jason Bateman, Portia de Rossi, and Will Arnett. Aired November 9, 2003, in broadcast syndication. 20th Century Fox, 2004, DVD.

Lane, Michael. "Don't Let Taxes Drag You Down." BlackRock Advisor Center. May 26, 2021. https://www.blackrock.com/us/financial-professionals/insights/preparing-portfolios-for-taxes.

Lee, Dennis. "When the Outlook is Blurry, Put on an After-Tax Lens." BlackRock Advisor Center. May 18, 2022. https://www.blackrock.com/us/financial-professionals/insights/after-tax.

Lincoln Financial Group. "The Underrated Impact of Taxes on Retirement." Accessed March 15, 2022, https://www.lfg.com/wcs-static/pdf/68%20percent%20The%20underrated%20impact%20of%20taxes%20on%20retireme.pdf.

LongTermCare.gov. "How Much Care Will You Need?" Accessed March 8, 2022. https://acl.gov/ltc/basic-needs/how-much-care-will-you-need.

Maverick, J. B. "S&P 500 Average Return." Investopedia. Last modified August 16, 2022. https://www.investopedia. com/ask/answers/042415/what-average-annual-return-sp-500.asp#toc-sp-500-historical-returns.

McLeod, Michael. "The History of Retirement." The Fiduciary Group Investment Managers. February 26, 2021. https://www.tfginvest.com/insights/the-history-of-retirement.

Munnell, Alicia H., Anqi Chen, and Robert L. Silciano. "National Retirement Risk Index: An Update from the 2019 SCF." *Center for Retirement Research at Boston College*, no. 21-2 (January 2021). https://crr.bc.edu/wp-content/uploads/2021/01/IB_21-2.pdf.

O'Leary, Angie, Griffin Geisler, and Daniel Gottlieb. "Taking Control of Healthcare in Retirement." RBC Wealth Management. Accessed March 8, 2022. https://www.rbcwealthmanagement.com/_assets/documents/insights/taking-control-of-health-care-in-retirement.pdf.

Pfau, Wade D., and Michael Finke. "Integrating Whole Life Insurance into a Retirement Income Plan: Emphasis on Cash Value as a Volatility Buffer Asset." The American College of Financial Services. April 2019. https://retirementincomejournal.com/wp-content/uploads/2020/03/WBC-Whitepaper-Integrating-Whole-Life-Insurance-into-a-Retirement-Income-Plan-Emphasis-on-Cash-Value-as-a-Volatility-Buffer-Asset.pdf.

PricewaterhouseCoopers. "Retirement in America: Time to Rethink and Retool." Accessed January 16, 2022. https://www.pwc.com/us/en/industries/financial-services/library/retirement-in-america.html.

Putnam Investments, "Social Security: Five Things You Need to Know." PowerPoint, PPT200 328161 12/21. Accessed

May 16, 2022. https://www.putnam.com/literature/pdf/ II937.pdf.

Stanford Center on Longevity. "Underestimating Years in Retirement." Accessed March 14, 2022. https://longevity. stanford.edu/underestimating-years-in-retirement/.

U.S. Bureau of Labor Statistics. "Databases, Table & Calculators by Subject." Accessed March 11, 2022. https://data.bls. gov/timeseries/CUUR0000SA0?amp%253bdata_tool =XGtable&output_view=data&include_graphs=true.

U.S. Inflation Calculator. "Historical Inflation Rates: 1914–2022." Accessed July 18, 2022. https://www.usinfla-tioncalculator.com/inflation/historical-inflation-rates/.

Webster, Ian. "Stock Market Returns Between 1957 and 2022." S&P 500 Data. Accessed January 25, 2022. https:// www.officialdata.org/us/stocks/s-p-500/1957.

AUTHOR BIO

Derek Mazzarella, CFP is a dedicated financial advisor committed to helping individuals achieve financial success. With a strong background in management from Bryant University, Derek's passion for assisting others lead him to become a Certified Financial Planner (CFP).

With a track record of serving hundreds of clients, Derek's financial acumen earned him the prestigious Five Star Wealth Professional recognition many times over. His financial insights have been featured on local news stations as well as reputable financial publications. Derek's commitment to his community is evident through his support of local nonprofits.

Outside of work, Derek treasures quality time with his family. He also enjoys playing soccer, basketball, and his guitar (although now it's mostly playing "Wheels on the Bus").

DISCLOSURES

Chapter 2:

Investing in Real Estate Investment Trusts (REITs) involves special risks such as potential illiquidity and may not be suitable for all investors. There is no assurance that the investment objectives of this program will be attained. International investing involves special risks such as currency fluctuation and political instability and may not be suitable for all investors. These risks are often heightened for investments in emerging markets. The prices of small cap stocks are generally more volatile than large cap stocks. The Standard & Poor's 500 Index is a capitalization weighted index of 500 stocks designed to measure performance of the broad domestic economy through changes in the aggregate market value of 500 stocks representing all major industries. Bonds are subject to market and interest rate risk if sold prior to maturity. Bond values will decline as interest rates rise and bonds are subject to availability and change in price. There is no guarantee that a diversified portfolio will enhance overall returns or outperform a non-diversified portfolio. Diversification does not protect against market risk. Stock investing includes risks, including fluctuating prices and loss of principal.

Chapter 9:

This information is not intended to be a substitute for specific individualized tax or legal advice. We suggest that you discuss your specific situation with a qualified tax or legal advisor.

Chapter 11:

There is no guarantee that a diversified portfolio will enhance overall returns or outperform a non-diversified portfolio. Diversification does not protect against market risk. Standard deviation is a historical measure of the variability of returns relative to the average annual return. If a portfolio has a high standard deviation, its returns have been volatile. A low standard deviation indicates returns have been less volatile.

Chapter 13

There is no guarantee that a diversified portfolio will enhance overall returns or outperform a non-diversified portfolio. Diversification does not protect against market risk. Variable Universal Life Insurance / Variable Life Insurance policies are subject to substantial fees and charges. Policy values will fluctuate and are subject to market risk and to possible loss of principal. Guarantees are based on the claims paying ability of the issuer. Both loans and withdrawals from a permanent life insurance policy may be subject to penalties and fees and, along with any accrued loan interest, will reduce the policy's account value and death benefit. Withdrawals are taxed only to the extent that they exceed the policy owner's cost basis in the policy and usually loans are free from current Federal taxation. A policy loan could result in tax consequences if the policy lapses or is surrendered while a loan is outstanding. Fixed Indexed Annuities (FIA) are not suitable for all investors. FIAs permit investors to participate in only a stated percentage of an increase in an index (participation rate) and may impose a maximum annual account value percentage increase. FIAs typically do not allow for participation in dividends accumulated on the securities represented by the index. Annuities are long-term, tax-deferred investment vehicles designed for retirement purposes. Withdrawals prior to 59 ½ may result in an IRS penalty, and surrender charges may apply. Guarantees are based on the claims-paying ability of the issuing insurance company. Bonds are subject to market and interest rate risk if sold prior to maturity. Bond values will decline as interest rates rise and bonds are subject to availability and change in price.

Milton Keynes UK
Ingram Content Group UK Ltd.
UKHW051827010224
437086UK00006B/53